HEALTH AND SAFETY COMMISSION/HOME OFFICE/ THE SCOTTISH OFFICE

GUIDE TO HEALTH, SAFETY AND WELFARE AT POP CONCERTS AND SIMILAR EVENTS

London: The Stationery Office

Applications for reproduction should be made in writing to The Copyright Unit, Her Majesty's Stationery Office, St Clements House, 2-16 Colegate, Norwich NR3 1BQ

Third impression 1998

ISBN 0 11 341072 7

Contents

PART III

FIRE SAFETY AND EMERGENCY PROCEDURES

PART IV

VENUE FACILITIES

MEMBERS OF THE WORKING PARTY

Members of the Health and Safety Executive Working Group

Mr R Limb	(N W Leicestershire District Council)
Mr P Rogerson	(London Borough of Newham)
Mr A Baker	(London Borough of Tower Hamlets)
Mr P Winsor	(Milton Keynes Borough Council)
Mr M Timlin	(London Borough of Lambeth)
Mr G Galilee	(London Borough of Brent)
Mr J Shaughnessy	(London Borough of Brent)
Mr R Parkins	(London Borough of Southwark)
Chief Inspector R Newman	(Essex Police)
Mr S Bullock	(Health and Safety Executive)
Mrs S Cowlin	(Health and Safety Executive)
Mr A Bell	(Health and Safety Executive)

Members of the Home Office Working Party

Miss V Jenson	(Fire Safety Division)
Mr G Hubbard	(Fire Safety Division)
Mr P Kilshaw OBE	(formerly Fire Service Inspectorate)
Mr E Burke	(Fire Service Inspectorate)
Mr M Carter	(Gwent Fire Brigade)

with advice contributed by the Home Office divisions responsible for licensing, the control of explosives, emergency planning and building works.

ACKNOWLEDGEMENTS

The Health and Safety Commission, the Home Office and The Scottish Office gratefully acknowledge the assistance provided by all who contributed to the consultation exercise which was carried out during the preparation of this guide. Also acknowledged is the kind permission of Midland Concert Promotions to reproduce certain photographs.

INTRODUCTION

About this guide and its aims

1. Pop concerts are increasing in number and technical complexity. For the purpose of this guidance they are events where live or recorded music of a modern popular nature is performed by solo or group performers before a live audience.

2. The guide aims to help those who organise these events so that they run safely. It has involved extensive consultation with concert promoters, venue managers, specialist trade associations, local authorities (who are responsible for licensing), and other relevant organisations.

3. The aim of the guide is to bring together into one document all the information needed by organisers and their contractors and employees to help them satisfy the requirements of the law. It will also enable them to understand the needs of others, particularly the emergency services and first aid organisations, with whom they will have to co-operate.

4. The guide distinguishes between legal requirements and advice on good practice by the appropriate use of such expressions as "must" (for a legal requirement) "should" or "will need to" where a need is either self evident or very strongly recommended, or "can" or other suitable language where what is being described is commonly accepted good practice.

5. Some events are larger and more complex than others. All are covered by legal requirements, but the additional things that may need to, or perhaps ought to, be done will differ according to the event. Readers will need to approach the guide in the spirit of taking from it the information which is suitable for their purposes.

6. Similarly, the guide will be useful to organisers of other events such as "raves", or classical music concerts held outdoors. Again, it will be necessary to apply the guidance to suit the circumstances. The guide is not however intended to be applied to events normally held at discotheques or nightclubs.

7. Organisers of events are not the only ones who will find the guide useful. One of its aims is to encourage consistency of approach among licensing authorities, health and safety inspectors and fire authorities. It provides basic standards and safety measures but leaves scope for a flexible approach taking into account the nature and size of the event.

8. The guide does not replace the need for potential licensees, event organisers or managers to seek advice where appropriate from competent persons, and particularly to consult the licensing authority well in advance. Nor does it replace the need for the licensing authority to consult the fire authority wherever it is appropriate to do so.

9. The guide is in four parts:–
- general advice on legal duties and on key points to event organisers;
- health and safety matters;

- fire safety matters; and
- venue facilities mainly covered under conditions of licence.

10. It tries throughout to make clear not just *what* is required but *why* it is necessary or sensible to do particular things, and particularly why licensing or fire authorities make certain demands. It has no statutory force, and is not an HSC Approved Code of Practice. However, the advice given is consistent with requirements in England and Wales and in Scotland under the Health and Safety at Work etc. Act 1974 (the HSW Act), the Fire Precautions Act 1971, the Building Regulations 1990 and the Building Standards (Scotland) Regulations 1990.

British, European and International Standards

11. Where references are made to British Standards in this Guide, these are technical standards published by the British Standards Institution. The standards are those in force at the time of publication. It should be noted that where a current British Standard is superseded by any European Standard published by the European Committee for Standardisation (CEN), the existing British Standard will either be withdrawn or the CEN Standard will be published by the British Standards Institution in their BS EN series.

PART I

THE ROLE OF THE

ORGANISER

Chapter 1

PLANNING AND ORGANISATION

Introduction

1.1 For the purpose of this chapter, the "organiser" is taken to be anyone who has a primary responsibility for the event, whether for its planning or for its management and supervision. In the case of many smaller events the same person will do both, and he or she may well also be an employer as well as a contractor.

1.2 The chapter can be read with advantage by anyone who has any part behind the scenes in "making the event go", but it is primarily aimed at those who have the main responsibilities and who therefore carry overall responsibility for safety.

Your legal duties

1.3 Arranging and running a pop concert counts as a "work activity" and is therefore subject to the Health and Safety at Work etc. Act 1974 (the HSW Act) and to the various regulations made under it. Anyone who is directly responsible for the undertaking, whether or not they are employers, will have responsibilities for the health and safety of third parties affected by it, including the audience; and if they are employers they will have responsibilities also for their employees.

1.4 You may also need an entertainment licence from the district, borough or islands council where the concert is to be held. Licensing authorities will place conditions on the event relating to its management, organisation and conduct.

1.5 You can find more information about your legal duties in Appendix 1, and Appendix 2 describes the enforcement of health and safety legislation.

Application of the guide

1.6 Venues such as concert halls and theatres which have obtained an entertainment licence from the local authority are likely to have agreed arrangements for many of the aspects of staging a pop concert.

1.7 However, a pop concert may also take place in circumstances where a licence is needed specifically for the event, or at venues which have not been designed for public entertainment, such as disused warehouses or aircraft hangars. It is in these circumstances that this guide will be particularly helpful.

1.8 The size and nature of the concert will also be important. If you are arranging a small, low risk event, you will find the main principles outlined in the guide will help you but you will not need to apply all the technical details which it contains. Assessing what the risks are for your particular event will therefore be important.

Planning

1.9 A safe and trouble-free event requires good planning. The investment you make in planning will be time well spent. For large events, experience shows that

6 to 9 months beforehand is not too early to start as licensing requirements and preparations by the emergency services take time. The early nomination of a safety co-ordinator for the event is highly desirable.

1.10 Good planning begins with evaluating both the *event* and the *venue*.

The event

1.11 The sort of questions you will need to consider about the event include:–

- what kind of audience will the event attract and what is their likely behaviour? Concerts attended by mainly young audiences can give rise to particular problems, such as hysteria;

- have similar events taken place which can give you useful information?

- are there aspects of the performance itself which may create risks?

- is there likely to be heavy alcoholic drinking? and

- how long will the event last? This will have implications for the facilities which will need to be provided and the number of stewards and other staff who will be necessary.

The venue

1.12 A concert can be held in a wide range of venues and the existing facilities, normally agreed by the licensing authority and the fire authority for established venues, will largely determine what needs to be done. The main questions you will need to think about are whether:–

- the means of escape/arrangements for emergency exits are adequate. This is particularly relevant for concerts held at venues not designed for public entertainment but will also need to be considered for regular venues if adaptations are made, such as the erection of temporary stands, or the admission of spectators to the pitch at a sports stadium; and

- if the concert is to be held outdoors, do the necessary facilities exist and if not, can they be provided? What are the implications of adverse weather conditions?

Event planning meetings

1.13 A good way of starting to plan for an event is to hold a meeting to bring together all the main interested parties.

1.14 An event planning meeting will be particularly useful if you are applying for a licence for a particular event. You may find that you need to hold several meetings if you are arranging a large event and the first meeting may need to be 3 to 6 months beforehand.

1.15 It is likely that the meetings will need to be attended by:–

- the event management team (e.g. venue owner, licensee/organiser, manager, event safety co-ordinator);

- representatives of departments of the local authority involved either as service providers or enforcers;

- representatives of the emergency services, emergency planning and transport services; and

- others providing services for the event (e.g. stewarding, first aid and welfare organisations and concessionaires) and any experts giving advice on, for example, noise levels, wind loading etc.

1.16 It is important for you to note agreed actions and circulate decisions in writing to all concerned.

1.17 The sort of information you are likely to need at an event planning meeting will include a site plan, technical drawings and data, sample materials, details of electrical and gas installations and an outline programme for the event.

Management structure

1.18 In many large concerts the practice is for the organiser to appoint a manager to be in charge of the event while themselves remaining responsible for the planning. There should, however, always be someone with the authority to act in place of the manager if this person has to leave the event.

1.19 At most concerts, the co-ordination and implementation of safety procedures are delegated to an individual, referred to in this guide as the event safety co-ordinator.

1.20 Whatever the management structure, you will need to decide who is responsible for the various safety duties, make sure that there are no overlaps or gaps and ensure that everyone knows their own responsibilities. These arrangements should be set down in writing. If several people are involved, there will need to be close liaison and good communication between them.

1.21 Whoever is acting as the event safety co-ordinator should also liaise with the chief steward, the emergency services, sub-contractors and any self-employed people to ensure that safety procedures are understood and followed.

Management of the event

1.22 The safe running of the event will be one of your main aims. A management system which enables you to anticipate, monitor and control potential risks can help you do this and can also help you meet your general legal obligations to protect the audience and workers as well as any licensing conditions.

1.23 The steps you will need to take to assess the risks associated with staging the event are set out in Appendix 1.

1.24 Before the audience enters the venue, the manager should check all fire and emergency facilities. The check should ensure that all exits are unlocked, escape routes are clear, emergency lighting works, and fire fighting equipment and alarms are fully working. The manager should also ensure that a public address system for use in emergencies can be heard clearly in all parts of the venue.

1.25 It may be helpful to arrange a safety announcement for the audience before the event starts. This could, for example, give information about the location of exits, the identification of stewards and procedures for evacuation.

1.26 During the concert, the manager should check that procedures are operating satisfactorily and take remedial action if problems are noted.

1.27 The sort of things that may indicate a deteriorating situation include:–

- significant crowd sway;

- treatment of a large number of casualties at first aid points;

- blocked or obstructed escape routes;

- excessive loadings or overcrowding on temporary structures;

- a build-up of waste which is not being removed; and

- inadequate maintenance of sanitary accommodation.

1.28 At large events, you will find it useful to have a procedure which enables the management team to liaise with local authority inspectors about public complaints. It is advisable to keep a log of complaints and to make a "hot-line" telephone number available for the public.

1.29 Organisers also often find it useful to have an "event log" which identifies checks which have been made and issues that have arisen. This log, which can take the form of a taped message, can then be used as part of the debriefing process, when the event is reviewed and evaluated.

1.30 Performers or their managers sometimes make requests for last minute changes to the plans for such items as the stage, the auditorium layout or rigs. If these affect the safety of the event, e.g. the escape routes, you will need to resist them. The sort of questions you should ask are:–

- do the changes reduce exit widths?

- do they reduce the available viewing area? and

- could they create narrow funnels which, in turn, could cause crushing?

1.31 Other changes to an agreed plan which are sometimes needed, in relation to car parking, movement of cars on or off site, or numbers of entrances should be implemented well in advance of the audience's arrival.

1.32 It may be helpful to hold progress meetings during the concert with key individuals or on a daily basis if the event is being held over a number of days.

Accident reporting

1.33 You will need to record all accidents. The best way of doing this is to ensure that the safety co-ordinator records the details in an accident book for the venue. Certain accidents must be reported to the relevant enforcing authority under the Reporting of Injuries, Diseases and Dangerous Occurrences Regulations 1985 using Form F2508. The leaflet HSE 11 (Rev) gives further information on reporting responsibilities and the injuries which must be reported. If a worker is injured, the employer has a statutory duty to make the report and in the case of a self-employed worker, either the individual, or somebody acting on his or her behalf, should make the report. If a member of the public is injured, the person with overall control of the venue, who is most likely to be the manager or the licensee, should make the report.

The rest of the guide

1.34 Parts II – IV of this guide give you the detailed information which will help you to run the event safely. They refer you to the regulations and standards you need to know and give advice or examples of good practice in other key areas.

1.35 Part II relates mainly to health and safety issues although for completeness, licensing or fire issues are sometimes included. It is split into two sections which cover crowd safety and venue standards. Some of the main points are set out in paragraphs 1.36 to 1.47.

Crowd safety

1.36 Protecting the safety of the audience is a central concern and to do this you will need to apply the best practices of health and safety management. Some of the important matters you will need to consider are covered in this section, for example:-

- how to assess the number of stewards who will be needed and the training and competences they should have (Chapter 3);

- arrangements for people with disabilities (Chapter 4);

- communication with the audience (Chapter 5); and

- the importance of a front of stage barrier and the standards this should meet (Chapter 6).

Venue standards

1.37 The failure of a temporary structure such as a stage, stand or marquee, could have devastating effects. The advice given in Chapters 7 and 8 on safety standards and the checks which should be made can help you to make sure that this does not happen.

1.38 Electrical installations at concert venues are often complicated and extensive, and special effects and pyrotechnics also require careful attention. You should therefore take proper precautions to avoid injury to workers, performers or the audience (see Chapters 9 and 10).

1.39 High sound levels can create a risk of permanent deafness. Chapter 11 summarises the requirements of the Noise at Work Regulations and gives you advice on controlling audience exposure to loud music. Appendix 3 also provides information about acoustical units and terminology.

1.40 Part III mainly concerns fire safety matters (for which the licensing authority may require detailed standards) and emergency procedures.

1.41 All venues need to be provided with adequate means of escape, adequate fire fighting equipment and appropriate means for giving warning in case of fire.

1.42 Chapters 12 to 15 give practical advice on these factors and also examine such matters as:–

- the maximum audience size (the "occupant capacity");

- exit and directional signs; and

- the use of curtains, drapes and artificial foliage.

1.43 Chapter 16 considers the arrangements which should be covered in emergency evacuation plans and the procedures that the emergency services follow if a major incident occurs.

1.44 It recommends that at large concerts an "incident control centre" should be set up for the use of personnel from the management team, the emergency services and other key organisations.

1.45 Part IV covers venue facilities which often have to meet conditions attached to licences.

1.46 In this part, you will find advice on:-

- planning traffic and transport arrangements (Chapter 17);

- assessing the medical and first aid provision which will be needed and who to consult (Chapter 18);

- welfare services and ways of giving information to the audience to help the event run smoothly (Chapter 19);

- food, refreshments and drinking water (Chapter 20);

- assessing how many sanitary conveniences will be needed and what standards they should meet (Chapter 21); and

- disposal of waste (Chapter 22).

1.47 The Appendices include more detailed information about the legislation which applies to pop concerts, guidance on who enforces health and safety legislation, with Appendix 4 providing a check list of items which you may find useful for your event.

NOTES/AMENDMENTS

PART II

CROWD SAFETY

AND

VENUE STANDARDS

Chapter 2

CROWD MANAGEMENT

Introduction

2.1   This chapter gives advice on audience safety. It looks in particular at audience size, entrances, seating, stairways, ramps, slopes and viewing areas.

Audience size: (the "occupant capacity")

2.2   The maximum size of the audience for a particular event is generally determined by the licensing authority (taking advice from the fire authority) and is known technically as the "occupant capacity". This will include all ticket holders, passholders and guests. The method for establishing this capacity is described in Chapter 13. The licensing authority may also place a restriction on the numbers allowed in certain parts of the venue. It is for the event organiser to ensure that the occupant capacity and any other specific restrictions are not exceeded.

2.3   The purpose of setting the occupant capacity is to ensure that the means of escape are adequate for the number of people attending the event. In the case of pop concerts, it also controls the numbers attending and thereby reduces crowd densities. Setting a number in this way also helps to identify other facilities which may be needed, e.g. first aid, stewards and sanitary conveniences.

2.4   Other than at small events, it is generally good practice for admission to be by ticket only. If tickets are to be sold at the event, there will need to be a ticket numbering and recording system so that a check can be made to ensure that the number sold beforehand plus those sold at the event do not exceed the occupant capacity. This will help the organiser to demonstrate quickly that the event is operating within agreed conditions.

2.5   A normal procedure is for tickets to be printed bearing a security code in order to prevent forgeries and the licensing authority may require an audited account of the number of tickets sold as a control check on the size of the audience. For safety reasons, and in order to ensure that the event is suitably managed, licensing authorities may require tickets to be issued for some concerts where admission is free.

Entry and exit points

2.6   The entrances to the venue provide the means for supervising, marshalling and directing the audience to the event. They also need to provide escape routes and immediate access for the emergency services during the concert.

2.7   In venues built for public entertainment, e.g. concert halls, theatres and sports stadia, the number of entrances and exits will have been approved at the design stage. In buildings not designed for public entertainment and at outdoor sites, there is a need for the number of entrances to be calculated in order to ensure that they are adequate for the occupant capacity (see Chapter 12).

2.8   Entrances and exits should be clearly signposted and operate efficiently. The needs of wheelchair users should be taken into account (see Chapter 4). Entrances and exits for pedestrian access should be separated from entry routes used by service and concession vehicles.

2.9 Problems may occur at entry points if large numbers of people seek to gain admission at the same time and if the situation is not properly managed, this may result in crushing injuries. It is therefore recommended that:–

- entrances are opened some considerable time (e.g. 1 to 2 hours) before the event is due to start and the audience is made aware of this by tickets, posters or other means. If significant crowding is likely to occur before that time, consideration can be given to opening gates in advance of the published time; and

- admission is staggered by providing early supporting acts or other activities.

2.10 Crowd pressure at the entrances can be further reduced by:–

- keeping all other activities including mobile concessions well clear of entry points;

- arranging for adequate queuing areas away from entrances;

- ensuring that barriers, fences, gates and turnstiles are suitable and sufficient for the numbers using them;

- locating ticket sales and pick-up points away from the entrance;

- providing a sufficient number of competent and trained stewards;

- arranging for a short-range public address system or a megaphone to be made available at entrances, in order that the public can be notified of any delay;

- providing for a filter system to ensure that prohibited items such as glass bottles, metal containers, alcohol, etc are not allowed into the venue; and

- arranging at outdoor events on green field sites, and particularly at large events, a system of free flow to help speed up entry to the venue (see suggested arrangements in diagram 1).

DIAGRAM 1: An example of free flow arrangements – a suggested layout

**GATE ENTRY PLAN FOR VENUES
WITH NO FIXED LANES**

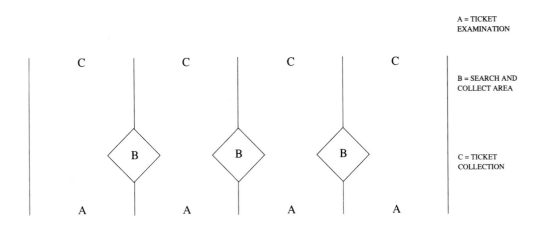

A = TICKET
EXAMINATION

B = SEARCH AND
COLLECT AREA

C = TICKET
COLLECTION

Summary:

PUBLIC ENTER BY ALL FOUR LANES. AT POINT "A" THEY ARE CHECKED FOR A VALID TICKET.

AT POINT "B" STEWARDS POSITIONED INSIDE THE DIAMOND CHECK FOR PROHIBITED ITEMS. ANYTHING TAKEN BY THE STEWARDS IS PLACED INSIDE THE DIAMOND AREA ALLOWING A CLEAR PATH THROUGH.

AT POINT "C" THE TICKET IS CHECKED.

CLEAN UP CREWS CLEAR THE DIAMONDS BY CLOSING ONE LANE AT A TIME WORKING ACROSS THE LANES.

THIS SYSTEM CAN OPERATE ON ANY AMOUNT OF LANES.

2.11 If people are likely to queue outside the venue for a considerable time, the organiser may need to provide suitable temporary sanitary accommodation. Arrangements should also be made to clear refuse in the area surrounding the venue.

Use of sports stadia for pop concerts

2.12 Turnstiles at sports stadia designated under the Safety of Sports Grounds Act 1975 are likely to have had detailed inspection by the relevant local authority. It is useful to note that the maximum notional rate through such turnstiles is 660 persons per hour.

2.13 Sports stadia issued with a general safety certificate under the Safety of Sports Grounds Act 1975 will already have adequate means of escape from the normal spectator areas. However, additional requirements will be needed if the pitch area is to be occupied by the public and/or by temporary structures, such as a stage or stands. If the stadium is designated under the 1975 Act a Special Safety Certificate will probably be required for the particular event. Where such a safety certificate is required the organiser will need to comply with specific terms and conditions. The local authority should therefore be consulted as early as possible.

Opening the gates and arrangements for the front of stage area

2.14 When gates are first opened at non-seated events, the audience tends to rush towards the front and this can cause tripping accidents and injuries. The organiser should therefore carefully consider how the area in front of the stage will be managed and stewarded when the gates are opened and if a standing area is provided in front of the stage, entrances should not lead directly to this area from stage right or left.

2.15 One recommended method of easing the initial crowding near the stage and preventing slipping or tripping accidents is to provide a line or lines of stewards across the arena through which the audience can move towards the stage in an orderly manner. This may be supplemented by public address announcements so that the audience is kept informed about what is happening. When the audience have reached the front of stage area it is helpful if they are encouraged to sit down. Problems can be caused if the audience is prevented from occupying the immediate front of stage area when they arrive.

Crowd sway or surges

2.16 The manager will need to monitor whether any crowd sway or surges present a risk to members of the audience. One way of achieving this at large concerts is to use closed circuit television. If the manager considers that individuals are at risk, he or she will need to take immediate action, e.g. by making an announcement and asking the performers to stop playing. If the performers notice crowd sway and surging they also can alert the crowd to the possibility of serious crushing injuries.

"Pass out" systems

2.17 "Pass out" systems, which allow people to temporarily leave the venue and then re-enter, are difficult to manage and largely depend on the security of the premises being used. Such a system should only be provided if suitable arrangements can be made to ensure that no unauthorised person is allowed access and that no prohibited items are allowed into the venue.

Perimeter fencing

2.18 At outdoor venues the provision of a fixed boundary will help the safe management of the crowd and prevent trespassers entering the site. For large events, a substantial perimeter fence may be needed. To ensure that such a fence is stable and can withstand large numbers of people pressing on it, it should be able to withstand a crowd loading of at least 2kN/m, tested at an appropriate height usually between 1.1 metres and 1.5 metres. It is also advisable for it to be at least 3 metres in height. At smaller events, a lesser height and lower loading standard may be satisfactory.

Admission of young children

2.19 It may not be appropriate to allow young children, particularly those under the age of 5, to attend certain events because they may be trampled or crushed. If they are not to be allowed in, this should be clearly advertised in advance. Where young children are allowed, the organiser should consider arrangements for prams and pushchairs, and at large events creche facilities may be useful.

Seating arrangements

2.20 Where an event is likely to attract an audience which is predominantly under the age of 16, there is a risk of over-excitement leading to hysteria. The organiser should consider holding an all-seated event for such audiences as this may help to prevent crowd surges and crushing at the front of stage area.

2.21 For an all-seated event, stewards should ensure that members of the audience do not stand on their seats or move into the gangways.

2.22 If temporary seating is provided, it will be necessary to ensure that the seating is adequately secured to avoid "snaking". The provision of loose seats is not recommended unless the seating area is very small (see paragraphs 7.72 to 7.74 for further advice on seating).

Stairways and ramps

2.23 When members of the audience go downstairs either at the end of an event, or in an emergency, problems can be caused by pressure from behind. Slipping and tripping frequently occurs on stairs and is more likely to happen in congested circumstances. To avoid this, stairways and ramps should have a uniform width, a non-slip surface and a shallow gradient. The width should be sufficient to allow free movement but narrow enough for people to reach a handrail. (See Chapter 12 for technical details).

Slopes

2.24 When venues have slopes in excess of 1 in 6, consideration should be given to the provision of exit steps or ramps with a non-slip surface. The area in front of the stage should be as flat as possible in order to prevent tripping and crushing.

Viewing area

2.25 It is important that an audience has a clear line of vision to the stage in order to avoid movement towards the centre. The widest possible sightlines from stage right to stage left help to reduce crowd density in front of the stage and help to minimise surging and the possibility of crushing injuries. The stage and "screamer" heights, sidestages and drapes should be positioned so as not to obscure views.

Note : A "screamer" is an elevated platform which runs from the centre of the stage to the extremity of stage right or left.

Video screens

2.26 At large concerts the organiser may want to use video or projection screens. Siting of screens near to the stage helps to stop those behind from pressing forward. At large outdoor events, it may be useful if screens are located some distance from the stage, as this will encourage a proportion of the audience to move to a less crowded part of the site. Not all types of screen operate in daylight and if the intention is to use a screen in these conditions, it will be necessary to ensure that an appropriate type is used.

2.27 The use of video screens to provide entertainment before the concert and during changeover periods can also help crowd management. They can also tell the audience about safety arrangements, facilities on the site, transport etc. However, screens may not be visible in all parts of the site and supplementary means of giving emergency information should be used.

NOTES/AMENDMENTS

STEWARDING

Introduction

3.1 This chapter explains the responsibilities and functions of stewards in relation to public safety and describes necessary training and competences.

3.2 The event organiser is responsible for ensuring that an adequate level of stewarding is provided at the venue. A chief steward is normally appointed to be responsible for the effective stewarding of the event.

Note: Organisers should appreciate that if for any reason matters get out of control, or if there is any kind of panic, everything will depend on calm and knowledgeable stewarding, directed as necessary from the incident control centre from which major announcements can be made.

Responsibilities and functions

3.3 The main responsibilities of stewards are crowd management, including the prevention of crushing. They are also there to assist the police and other emergency services should the need arise. The training and competences necessary for stewards at a particular event will depend on the duties to be undertaken.

3.4 Stewards' functions include:-

- working in the "pit" area;

- ensuring security at entrances or exits;

- minimising the risk of fire by carrying out fire patrols; and

- controlling vehicle parking and marshalling traffic.

3.5 Performers may have their own security arrangements and a clear division of responsibility needs to be agreed between such security personnel and stewards.

Deployment and numbers of stewards

3.6 In order to manage the audience it is important for stewards to be located at *key points*. These include barriers, the pit areas, gangways, entrances and exits and the mixer desk and delay towers.

3.7 The organiser should ensure that a comprehensive survey is carried out to assess the parts of the venue where stewards will be needed and identify the number of stewards required to manage the audience. Basing the assessment on a survey rather than on a precise mathematical formula allows full account to be taken of all relevant circumstances, including previous experience.

Indoor events

3.8 For audiences mainly over 16 a useful guide is:-

- a minimum of 1 steward for every 100 members of the audience without seating; or

- a minimum of 1 steward for every 250 members of the audience where permanent fixed seating is provided.

3.9 If most of the audience are under 16, more stewards will be required. For example, the licensing authority may require 2 stewards for every 100 members of the audience if it is an event without seating.

3.10 The figures in paragraphs 3.8 and 3.9 do not take into account stewards needed for car parking and traffic marshalling duties.

3.11 It is likely that additional stewards will be needed if the venue is not designed for public assembly. It should also be remembered that stewards will be needed for each entrance or exit.

Outdoor events

3.12 To calculate the number of stewards needed for outdoor events, it is suggested that each separate task is considered and the numbers required then added together. An important factor is that each exit should have at least 1 steward for the duration of the event but more when the event opens and closes. A high ratio of stewards is likely to be required where, for example:–

- previous experience has shown that audiences may exhibit undisciplined behaviour; or

- uneven ground creates difficulties with access and egress; or

- the site has an extensive perimeter fence and a large number of entry and exit points.

Organisation of stewards

3.13 There has to be an established chain of command. The arrangements will depend on the nature and size of the event and venue but may include:–

- a chief steward who liaises with the event manager and safety co-ordinator;

- a number of senior supervisors, responsible for different tasks, who report directly to the chief steward; and

- a number of supervisors who report direct to a senior supervisor and who are normally in charge of 6 to 10 stewards.

Stewards and their role

3.14 All stewards need to be fit to undertake the duties allocated to them (normally aged between 18 to 55 for the more physical tasks). While on duty they should:–

- concentrate only on their duties and not on the performance;

- not leave their place without permission;

- not consume or be under the influence of alcohol; and

- remain calm and be courteous towards members of the audience.

3.15 Stewards should not be stationed for long periods near to loudspeakers and arrangements should be made for them to have rest periods at reasonable intervals.

3.16 All stewards should wear distinctive clothing, such as tabards and be individually identifiable by means of a name or number.

Training and competences

3.17 It is recommended that stewards receive a written statement of their duties, a check-list, if this is appropriate, and a plan showing key features. They should receive briefing prior to the event, particularly about communicating with supervisors and others in the event of an emergency.

3.18 It is important that stewards are competent. Duties and competences include:–

- knowing the layout of the site and being able to assist the public by giving information about the available facilities, remembering the needs of people with disabilities;

- being aware of the location of entrances and exits and first aid points;

- ensuring that no overcrowding occurs in any part of the venue by managing and directing the audience particularly on entering or leaving the venue;

- keeping gangways and exits clear at all times and preventing standing on seats and furniture;

- controlling unruly behaviour and investigating immediately any disturbances or incidents;

- ensuring that combustible refuse does not accumulate;

- communicating with the incident control centre in the event of an emergency; and

- knowing and understanding the arrangements for evacuating the audience, including coded messages and undertaking specific duties in an emergency.

3.19 All stewards should be trained to carry out their duties effectively and the type of training will depend on the functions to be performed. A record should be kept of the training and instruction provided. All stewards, unless their duties are solely concerned with controlling parking and marshalling traffic, need to be trained in fire safety matters, emergency evacuation and dealing with incidents such as bomb threats. For those working in the pit area training should be given to ensure that they are able to lift distressed persons out of the audience safely and without risk to themselves.

3.20 Fire safety training should include the following:–

- the action to take on discovering a fire;

- how to raise the alarm, and the procedures this sets in motion;

- the action to be taken upon hearing the fire alarm;

- the procedures for alerting members of the public including, where appropriate, directing them to exits;

- the arrangements for calling the fire brigade;

- the evacuation procedures for the venue to an assembly point at a place of safety;

- the location and use of fire fighting equipment;

- the location of the escape routes, including those not in regular use;

- how to open all escape doors;

- the importance of keeping fire doors closed;

- how to stop machines and processes and isolate power supplies where appropriate;

- the reason for not using lifts (other than those specifically provided or adapted for use by people with disabilities in accordance with British Standard 5588: Part 8); and

- the importance of general fire precautions and good housekeeping.

3.21 The manager or individual responsible for the training of stewards should keep records of all fire safety training. The record should include:–

- the date of the instruction or exercise;

- the duration;

- the name of the person giving the instruction;

- the name of the person(s) receiving the instruction; and

- the nature of the instruction, training or drill.

Note: Some fire authorities provide training courses for stewards.

Additional training required for supervisory staff

3.22 All supervisory staff should be trained in the handling of emergencies and should understand the limits of their responsibility which will have been defined with the emergency services at the planning stage. Supervisors should be familiar with the communications system for the event and the working of the incident control centre (see Chapter 16). It is advisable for some of the supervisory staff to have received training in first aid, particularly in cardiac pulmonary resuscitation.

Observation points

3.23 At major outdoor concerts at least two observation points are needed and these should be staffed throughout the event. Stewards at these points should have a clear view of the audience and be able to communicate with the incident control centre at all times. Head-sets or earphones will help to overcome general background noise.

Plan of venue

3.24 Organisers should have a plan of the venue to assist the general management of the event and the arrangements for any emergency.

Professional security advice

3.25 There are a number of specialist security companies. If such a company is used, it is recommended that the organiser should check that it:–

- carries adequate public and employer liability insurance;

- maintains accurate personnel files;

- has a company policy on health and safety;

- has a company code of conduct; and

- employs an adequate number of personnel who are competent in the following areas:–

  - fire safety and emergency evacuation

  - basic first aid; and

  - communication procedures.

NOTES/AMENDMENTS

Chapter 4

FACILITIES FOR PEOPLE WITH DISABILITIES

Introduction

4.1 Organisers of pop concerts should make suitable arrangements, wherever possible, to ensure that people with disabilities are able to attend. These include wheelchair users, those who have difficulty in walking, and those with impaired vision or hearing. Details of national organisations who may provide guidance are given in paragraph 4.11.

Access

4.2 At the planning stage, the event organiser needs to consider how people with disabilities can best be accommodated. Provisions should include easy access and adequate means of escape for use in an emergency. The number who can be admitted will need to be agreed with the licensing authority and will be dependent upon a number of factors including the structural and internal layout of the venue. The provision of wheelchair spaces in different parts of the seating area helps wheelchair users to sit with friends and have a choice of location.

Note: Wheelchair spaces in parts of the seating area should allow adequate room for manoeuvring a wheelchair. Generally, a manual wheelchair needs approximately 0.9 metres width x 1.4 metres depth. An electric wheelchair will need more space.

4.3 When someone transfers from a wheelchair to a seat, provision needs to be made for the wheelchair to be readily accessible without it causing an obstruction in a gangway or exit route. Where a disabled person remains in their wheelchair, the wheelchair should be placed in a position where it will not obstruct other people in an emergency and where a ready means of escape is available. It is useful for a steward to be available to assist in an emergency.

4.4 Wheelchair users cannot usually negotiate steps without help from the able bodied. This means that access and internal routes should be either on the level or by way of ramps.

4.5 Ramps for wheelchair users should conform to British Standard 5810. The ramp should have an easy gradient and it is suggested that this should be no steeper than 1 in 12. Ramps should have level resting space landings every 10 metres. They should also have raised safety edges and handrails.

4.6 A standing audience can cause surging movements and all wheelchair users should therefore be located in an area where they will not be affected, and will have a clear view of the stage.

4.7 At outdoor concerts wheelchair users should, wherever possible, be accommodated either in an open area or on a flat terrace. The following points should also be considered:–

- setting aside areas which give a clear view of the stage (the eye level of a wheelchair user is estimated as being between 1.1 metres and 1.25 metres);

- providing firm surfaces for access, escape routes and viewing areas;

- providing direct access to an exit; and

- where dense crowds are likely, accommodating people with disabilities on a special viewing platform.

People with impaired vision

4.8 People with impaired vision or colour perception may have difficulty in recognising information signs including those used for fire safety. Signs therefore need to be designed and sited so that they can easily be seen and are readily distinguishable. Good lighting and the use of simple colour contrasts can also help visually impaired people find their way around. Advice on any of these matters may be obtained from the Royal National Institute for the Blind or the National Federation of the Blind of the United Kingdom.

Venue suitability

4.9 In deciding whether a venue is suitable for people with disabilities, wheelchair users should be specially considered, as should the accessibility of facilities (such as refreshments and sanitary accommodation), the legibility of signs, and quality of lighting. Suitable, identified car parking should also be available near the venue with spaces wider than normal (about 3.6 metres) to allow room for manoeuvre.

Publicity

4.10 It is helpful if organisers publicise the facilities which are available by contacting, as appropriate:–

- the local disability association, access group and any local clubs or organisations for people with disabilities;

- national organisations for people who are disabled who can distribute information to their branches throughout the country;

- the local authority social services department in the appropriate area;

- local newspapers and radio stations, including talking newspapers;

- tourist boards and tourist information centres; and

- "In Touch" and "Does He Take Sugar", BBC radio programmes for the blind and disabled, which reach a wide audience and provide an important information exchange.

Sources of advice

4.11 Names and addresses of organisations representing disabled and sensory-impaired people can be found in Yellow Pages. For convenience, some of the principal organisations concerned are as follows:–

- Access Committee for England, 25 Mortimer Street, London W1N 8AB (071 637 3037)

- The Association of Access Officers , c/o Wrekin District Council, PO Box 212, Malinsee House, Telford, Shropshire TF3 4LL (0952 203036)

- British Council of Organisations of Disabled People, de Bradelei House, Chapel Street, Belper, Derbyshire DE56 1AR (0773 828182)

- Centre for Accessible Environments, 35 Great Smith Street, London SW1P 3BJ (071 222 7980)

- Disability Scotland, Princes House, 5 Shandwick Place, Edinburgh EH2 4RG (031 229 8632)

- Disabled Living Foundation, 380-384 Harrow Road, London W9 2HU (071 289 6111)

- Joint Committee on Mobility for Disabled People, Woodcliff House, 51a Cliff Road, Weston-Super-Mare, Avon BS22 9SE (0934 642313)

- MENCAP, National Centre, 123 Golden Lane, London, EC1Y ORT (071 454 0454)

- MIND, 22 Harley Street, London, W1N 2ED (071 446 1654)

- National Federation of the Blind of the United Kingdom, Unity House, Smyth Street, Westgate, Wakefield, West Yorkshire WF1 1ER (0924 291313)

- National Music and Disability Information Service, Dartington Hall, Totnes, Devon TQ9 6EJ (0803 866701)

- RADAR (Royal Association for Disability and Rehabilitation), 25 Mortimer Street, London W1N 8AB (071 637 5400)

- Royal National Institute for the Blind, 224 Great Portland Street, London W1N 6AA / 10 Magdala Crescent, Edinburgh EH12 5BF (071 388 1266 / 031 313 1498)

- Royal National Institute for Deaf People, Science and Technology Unit, 105 Gower Street, London WC1E 6AH / 9 Clairmont Gardens, Glasgow G3 7LW (071 387 8033 / 041 332 0343)

- Wales Council for the Disabled, Llys Ifor, Crescent Road, Caerphilly, Mid Glamorgan CF8 1XL (0222 887325)

NOTES/AMENDMENTS

COMMUNICATION

Introduction

5.1 Communication, particularly during a large event, is of major importance. Each organisation involved in the running of the event, e.g. the management team, stewards, first aiders, the local authority and the emergency services (police, fire and ambulance) will have its own chain of command and communication arrangements. There needs to be clear and effective communication between the various disciplines and identified lines of demarcation. At the planning stage, it is therefore important to agree in writing the procedures, roles and specific duties of each organisation. The police, the management team and stewards need to ensure that there is an effective way in which they can communicate with each other so that in the event of an emergency, procedures are co-ordinated.

Radio

5.2 If radio communication is used, the following points should be taken into account:-

- all large events should have a properly organised operations centre (normally the incident control centre) adequately staffed by competent and trained radio operators. Representatives of the emergency services should have access to and use of this centre;

- all channels or frequencies should be submitted to the event organiser prior to the event and records of these kept in the radio operations centre;

- key channels or frequencies such as those for the management team and stewards should be monitored and conversations logged;

- users of radios should be trained in their use prior to the event;

- the power supply to any base control unit should be protected against failure of the on site electrical power supply;

- radios should be tested prior to the concert (with tests being carried out not less than 100m from the base control unit) and once the audience has arrived;

- individual call signs should be used;

- established radio procedure should be followed;

- operators stationed in noisy areas should use earphones;

- coded messages should be used in an emergency situation, and radio silence maintained by non-essential users;

- for portable radios, a fully-charged battery should be installed prior to the event and a fully-charged spare battery should be carried;

- a charging facility for batteries is useful if the event extends over a number of days; and

- operators should have regular rest periods.

Note: Radio equipment should be operated under the terms of a licence issued under the Wireless Telegraphy Act 1949.

Communications with the public

5.3 The event manager needs to be able to communicate with the audience. This can be accomplished by the use of clear and frequent public address announcements and supplemented by the use of video screens and by the provision of conspicuous signs. An information point and/or a lost persons meeting point may also be helpful.

Public address system

5.4 Broadcast music should be capable of being silenced in the event of an emergency. It should be under the direct control of a competent person who is trained in the emergency procedure for the venue, be capable of being controlled from the incident control centre and be accessible to the emergency services. It is important that messages transmitted over the public address system are clearly audible in all parts of the venue.

5.5 Wiring of the system should be routed through areas of low fire risk and protected where necessary against mechanical damage and interference by unauthorised persons. Where a permanent system is provided the wiring should be installed in accordance with British Standard 5839: Part 1. The power supply for the system should ensure continuous operation in the event of a failure of the mains power system. British Standard 7443 specifies the requirements for sound systems used in the event of an emergency.

5.6 At large outdoor events, a public address system outside the venue can be of assistance in providing information to the audience.

5.7 Loud hailers should be available for use by stewards and police.

Compere or DJ

5.8 A compere or DJ, who has empathy with the audience, may be able to relay appropriate information. It can be helpful for a compere or DJ to be on stage from the time doors/gates open to assist in crowd management, particularly at the front of stage area.

5.9 During the concert, performers may also be able to give warnings to the audience, particularly if they consider that crushing could occur.

NOTES/AMENDMENTS

Chapter 6

BARRIERS

Introduction

6.1 Barriers at pop concerts serve several different purposes. They can provide physical security, as in the case of a high perimeter fence at an outdoor concert, or be used to prevent the audience climbing on top of mixer towers, etc. They may also be used to relieve and prevent the build up of crowd pressures. For example, a properly constructed front of stage barrier enables those suffering physical distress to be reached and helped more easily.

6.2 Barriers will always be subject to crowd loading and should therefore be designed to withstand right angle and parallel loads commensurate with the probable pressures. Account should be taken of the nature of the loading, e.g. surging.

Front of stage barrier

6.3 The licensing authority may require a front of stage barrier as a condition of licence, particularly if significant crowd pressure is expected. The organiser should, in any case, assess whether such a barrier is needed and what form it should take. Factors to be taken into account include crowd density, the likely behaviour and size of the audience and the nature of the venue. For most large concerts some form of front of stage barrier will be required.

6.4 Crowd pressure is normally greatest at the front of stage barrier. If the crowd surges, dynamic loads may be considerable, but such pressure is momentary and to date has not been identified as the cause of serious injury. First aid treatment from crowd pressure will normally be for fainting and exhaustion often due, in part, to other factors (heat, alcohol, hysteria, etc). However, there is a risk that a crowd may "collapse" due to surging or heaving motions near its front resulting in people falling to the ground and being trampled and perhaps asphyxiated. A suitably designed and constructed barrier arrangement can help to reduce the risk of collapse.

6.5 The barrier needs to be at an appropriate height on the audience side to prevent thoracic compression. It is suggested that this should be no less than 1.1 metres from the surface on which the audience stands. Many barriers are constructed at 1.2 metres but this height is sometimes reduced for a very young audience.

The "Pit"

6.6 The area between the stage and the front of stage barrier (the "pit") should be designed to assist the work of stewards, first aiders and paramedics. An important role of stewards is to extract members of the audience who are in distress. The pit should have a non-slip unobstructed working area behind the barrier which is large enough to allow those in the pit to lift members of the audience into it. Some form of elevated platform inside the barrier can help with the lifting of people and enable stewards to oversee the audience and identify anyone in distress. Entrances or exits from the pit should be unobstructed to allow stretcher bearers clear access to a medical or first aid point away from the pit area. It is also helpful if pit exits are at least 1.1 metre wide.

6.7 Any arrangements for TV film crew or photographers to work in the pit area should be agreed with the event manager who will need to be satisfied that their activity will not interfere with the work of stewards or first aid staff.

6.8 A concert held "in the round" with a standing audience requires special arrangements for a pit area. The provision of an unobstructed escape corridor enables members of the audience taken over the barrier to be led away from the pit. However, care needs to be taken to avoid creating a point where people can be trapped between the escape corridor and the barrier.

Types of front of stage barrier construction

6.9 There are various types of barrier in use in the entertainment industry. Three examples are:-

- an "A" frame scaffold barrier (tube and couplers) which normally has a 1 metre tread plate at the front and may be fixed to the stage to prevent lateral movement;

- a demountable barrier system, which is custom built for the purpose and easily transported. These systems are also "A" framed and rely on a tread plate at the front to maintain their stability. They are normally free standing but if used outdoors may be fixed to the stage structure with couplers. Fixing by couplers is only appropriate if the stage is designed to resist the imposed lateral load; and

- a barrier constructed from staging sections with additional bracing to meet the loading requirements. These may be box section steel structures.

6.10 Scaffold barriers should be "system designed" to meet the necessary loadings. Checks should be made by a competent person to ensure that, when erected, the barrier meets the design criteria. If it is to be used for subsequent concerts, it is recommended that a check be made prior to each event to ensure that couplers are tight and that there are no signs of movement or damage to the structure.

6.11 To prevent injuries from barriers, the following questions should be answered:-

- is padding provided on all exposed couplers which might cause injury?

- are metal barriers smooth with no rough edges or trapping points, either when in position or when under load? To ease the lifting of members of the audience, has the barrier a smooth curved timber or steel top or is the top of the front plate or board padded?

- have steps been taken to ensure that there are no sharp or protruding objects from the barrier, eg bolts? and

- do barriers which have a tread plate or floor panel have a ramped approach or other similar arrangement to reduce the risk of tripping?

6.12 There should be a reasonable distance between the front barrier and the edge of the stage. It should in no circumstances be less than 1 metre and should often be more, or outdoors considerably more.

Barrier loadings

6.13 British Standard 6180 "Code of Practice for protective barriers in and about buildings" contains detailed guidance about the general design and construction of temporary and permanent protective barriers. These technical standards are appropriate for pop concerts. Barrier loading and construction will need to take account of a number of factors including the venue, the size and nature of the audience, artificial breaks created within the audience, performers' anticipated behaviour, etc.

6.14 At indoor venues, barriers and their integral components should be able to withstand a minimum loading of 3kN/m right angle load tested 10cm below the top. At outdoor events, the minimum loading should be increased to 5kN/m right angle load. These recommended standards may need to be varied, depending on the size of the audience, the nature of the venue and the anticipated crowd loading.

Shape of the front of stage barrier

6.15 If a venue has restricted space, a straight barrier is suitable. However, for large concerts, particularly those outdoors, a convex barrier extending into the audience may be preferable. In such circumstances, the barrier should consist of short, straight sections installed at angles to each other to form a curve across the main performance area, extending to the ends of the sidestages. It should be erected in conjunction with escapes to right and left of the stage. Concave stage barriers should not be used as these create areas where people can be trapped, although at certain events a "finger" barrier may be appropriate (see paragraph 6.21).

6.16 A curved barrier can provide the following additional safety benefits at large events:–

- it dissipates crowd surges away from the centre of the stage;

- it assists means of escape;

- it provides a wider front row sightline;

- it improves security by placing a greater distance between the downstage edge and the barrier making it difficult for fans to reach the stage; and

- it can provide a wider area for stewards and first aiders to operate within the "pit".

Barrier around thrusts

6.17 Where thrusts extend into the audience, a barrier should be provided in one of the following ways:–

- a stewarded barrier complying with the design criteria and loading factors for a front of stage barrier (see also paragraphs 6.9 to 6.14); or

- a scaffold structure close boarded to a height of 2.4 metres and designed to comply with the required crowd loading standard (see paragraph 6.14).

Note: A "thrust" is a section of the stage which projects from the main body of the stage towards the audience.

6.18 It is advisable to construct a thrust in such a way that it does not create poor sightlines. Care should be taken to ensure that such stage designs do not result in concave trapping points from which crowds cannot escape. This may be avoided by providing short exit tunnels beneath such thrusts.

Sidestage barrier or fences

6.19 The construction of a high sidestage barrier will form a sightline obstruction and will therefore ensure that important exits to the right and left of the stage are kept clear and available for use in an emergency. Such a barrier should always be provided for standing audiences and may need to be 6 metres in length (for wide outdoor concert stages) and 2.4 metres in height. Sidestage barrier loadings should comply with British Standard 6180.

Additional barrier arrangements

6.20 At large outdoor events, it may be possible to have an additional barrier arrangement to reduce the likelihood of crowd collapse (see paragraph 6.4). This could take the form of a "finger" barrier, extending into the audience (see paragraph 6.20) or, at sports stadia, a multiple barrier arrangement (see paragraphs 6.21 to 6.26).

Finger barrier

6.21 If a finger barrier is used, careful design is needed to avoid the creation of trapping points. The barrier should be able to withstand the same crowd loading as the front of stage barrier and should have an area which meets the recommendations set out in paragraph 6.6 and which enables stewards and first aiders to have access to the audience along its length.

Multiple barrier arrangements

6.22 For events held in sports stadia, it may be possible to use a multiple barrier system (i.e. double or triple barriers in front of the stage). If it is proposed to use such a system, escape arrangements will need to be agreed with the licensing authority.

6.23 Multiple barrier systems are not suitable for all venues and would be difficult and expensive to arrange on green field sites. For instance controlled side escapes, which are likely to be possible in sports stadia, would be difficult to arrange at other venues. Penning of audiences in flat, open areas by means other than the arrangements described in paragraphs 6.23 to 6.26 (i.e. a multiple barrier system) could also create difficulties in evacuation and is considered to be unsafe.

6.24 Where double or triple barrier arrangements are used, the barriers should form a convex curve into the audience with escapes from both ends. Because of the length of barrier required, it is only practical to use a demountable system.

6.25 The provision of a corridor or area behind each curved barrier will give stewards and first aiders adequate access to the public along the length of the barriers. The barriers used to achieve this should meet the required minimum loading (see paragraph 6.14).

6.26 Multiple barrier systems require careful management. One way of monitoring the numbers admitted is to issue a fixed number of colour coded wrist bands (one colour for each area) to the audience, corresponding to the capacity of each area.

6.27 With an over-enthusiastic audience, it is likely that many of the problems normally encountered at the front of stage barrier will be experienced at the barrier furthest from the stage. It is therefore essential that adequate numbers of first aiders and stewards are provided. However, because of the wider sightline potential (75% in some cases) and the increased distances from the stage, the incidence of crowd surge and crushing may be reduced.

Chapter 7

TEMPORARY STRUCTURES

Introduction

7.1 This chapter gives guidance on the design and erection of the many temporary structures associated with a pop concert. The failure of any temporary structure in a crowded, confined space could have devastating effects. It is therefore essential to plan, monitor, and erect structures using safe working practices. The chapter first gives guidance for all types of temporary structure and then considers factors which are relevant to certain specific structures.
Structures include:-

- the stage;
- dance platforms;
- towers and masts; and
- temporary stands and viewing platforms.

PLANNING

Design and load calculations

7.2 Construction drawings will normally be required for all temporary structures. These should be accompanied by full calculations, design loads and any relevant test results. For venues which hold a permanent licence, these details should normally be sent to the licensing authority at least 14 days before the event. For events which require an occasional licence, the licensing authority will need them at least 14 days before construction commences. It is however preferable for all such details to be submitted with the licence application. The health and safety enforcing authority may also wish to see the construction drawings, calculations and any test results.

7.3 There are two possible ways of calculating the design loads on a structure. The first is to use British Standard 6399 if this is relevant to the circumstances.

The second is to undertake an assessment. If this is to be done for dead loads, a self-weight of the structure and all the equipment to be placed on it needs to be assessed and multiplied by a partial safety factor of 1.4. For live loads, the assessment needs to cover the loads likely to be imposed when it is in use ie by people using or working on the structure, multiplied by a partial safety factor of 1.6.

7.4 In relation to temporary stands the Institution of Structural Engineers' publication "Safety Considerations for the Design and Erection of Demountable Grandstands" gives advice on assessing stability. It also gives advice on the forces arising from crowd movement, which can cause instability and collapse of a stand if they are not adequately taken into account and allowed for. If flags, hoardings, signs, etc. are to be attached to a stand these need also to be considered in the assessment of such structures and it is recommended that the advice of a competent engineer is sought as wind loads are likely to be increased.

Ground/floor loads

7.5 The event organiser should obtain information about the load bearing capacity of the ground or floor. For outdoor events the organiser should ensure that the ground load bearing capacity is capable of supporting the imposed loadings in all weather conditions.

7.6 The following factors may influence the choice of location for temporary structures:-

- whether the site is adequately drained. The site should not be liable to flooding which could either cause the load bearing capacity of the structure to be reduced or wash away the ground under the supports;

- whether the site is flat or can be made flat. Where there is a gradient or the ground is uneven, the structure needs to be capable of being modified to deal with such variations;

- whether there are overhead power cables, and if present whether they are sufficiently clear of the upper part of the structure; and

- whether the proximity of surrounding buildings, structures and vegetation creates risks in relation to the possible spread of fire.

7.7 After the structure has been erected the ground should be checked regularly to confirm that no deterioration in its load bearing capacity, such as excessive settlement, has occurred.

Legislation

7.8 The Management of Health and Safety at Work Regulations 1992 set out broad general duties which apply to almost all work activities. They are designed to encourage a more systematic and better organised approach to dealing with health and safety. The Regulations require employers to assess the risk to health and safety and use the most appropriate means of reducing those risks to an acceptable level.

7.9 Where personal protective equipment is assessed to be the most effective means of controlling the risk of injury, employers must issue this to workers, advise on its use and ensure that it meets the requirements of the Personal Protective Equipment (Safety) Regulations 1992. This equipment includes safety helmets, safety footwear, waterproof clothing, gloves, eye and ear protectors. "Pit" safety helmets may not be suitable in all cases and where not appropriate a reduced peak helmet or a mountain helmet may be acceptable. Flexible headbands and chin straps can help to secure the helmet and enhance comfort.

7.10 The Manual Handling Operations Regulations 1992 have replaced all existing legislation on the lifting and carrying of loads and came into force on 1 January 1993. They set out new requirements for safe handling of loads and people where there is a risk of injury and cover all hazardous manual handling operations.

7.11 The main duties of employers are to:-

- so far as is reasonably practical, avoid the need for manual handling of operations involving a risk of injury;

- assess the risk of injury in those operations that cannot be avoided; and

- reduce the risk of injury to the lowest level reasonably practicable, using the assessment as a basis for action.

The assessment must take into account a number of factors including the load, the task, the working environment and individual capability. To aid employers, HSE has published general guidance on the Regulations.

7.12 The assembly of temporary stands and viewing platforms is regulated by the Construction (General Provisions) Regulations 1961, the Construction (Working Places) Regulations 1966, and the Construction (Lifting Operations) Regulations 1961.

7.13 The Construction (Design and Management) Regulations will take effect by 1 January 1994. These are expected to place a duty on the event organiser, designers, contractors and self employed persons involved in construction projects to minimise risks to workers and to others.

MONITORING BY SAFETY CO-ORDINATOR

7.14 All activities at the venue relating to the erection and construction of temporary structures should be monitored by the event safety co-ordinator to ensure that safe working practices are followed and that temporary structures are erected to the detailed specification. A "hand-over" certificate ensures that the work has been carried out to a satisfactory standard using suitable materials. The enforcing authority may also require a copy of a method statement for the system of work used for erecting the particular structure.

7.15 The safety co-ordinator should ensure that all structures are checked by a competent person after they have been erected and before they are used, to make sure that they conform with the drawings and specified details. If this check is carried out by a person employed by the contractor erecting the structure, the safety co-ordinator should verify that the checks have been carried out effectively and have been recorded. The structure should comply fully with the design criteria before the public are admitted to the site. If modifications to the structures are necessary, the safety co-ordinator should liaise with the licensing authority.

ERECTING STRUCTURES

Safe working practices

7.16 A method statement should be drawn up for the erection of any structure.

7.17 Excavation work should be undertaken in such a way that the digging of trenches does not affect the stability of structures. For example trenches should not be dug near any stanchions in such a way that they undermine or adversely affect stability. Unfilled trenches can also be hazardous and should be covered with a suitable material, capable of withstanding any loads to which they may be subjected and fixed so that the material cannot be inadvertently dislodged. The sides of all trenches of 1.2 metres or deeper should be fully supported to prevent collapse or significant ground movement. Further guidance is contained in HSE Summary Sheet 558 - Safety in Excavations.

7.18 Structures should be erected from either the ground or from suitable stable platforms, mobile working platforms or ladders. HSE guidance note GS-42 "Tower Scaffolds" gives further advice.

7.19 If a scaffold is to be used by any person other than those erecting it, access ways such as ladders will be needed. Suitable provisions should be made for the areas which will need to be accessed once the structure has been built.

7.20 HSE guidance note GS-31 "Safe use of Ladders" sets out simple procedures for those using ladders. In particular, it recommends that where ladders are used they should be firmly secured and extend to at least 1 metre above the working platform and be placed at an angle of 75° to the horizontal.

7.21 Whilst structures are being erected, it is advisable not to lift materials over the heads of people working or passing below. It is therefore good practice to create "no go" areas below working areas from which other employees and members of the public are excluded.

7.22 Guard rails should normally be provided where a drop exceeds 2 metres. If this is not practicable, an alternative is to provide safety nets or a safety harness which can protect workers from falling off working platforms.

7.23 If guard rails are provided, the addition of toe-boards can enhance safety. Side netting may also be needed where there is a risk of items falling onto people below. Where netting is provided, it should be capable of preventing a spherical object of 100mm in diameter from passing through it.

7.24 Equipment should be checked to ensure that it is fit for its purpose and fully meets any specification which has been laid down. For example, steel items with cracked welds, bent or buckled members, or with large amounts of rust should be rejected.

7.25 All components should be examined during assembly and dismantling for signs of wear, deformation or other damage, and replaced where necessary. Correct alignment of components is important - they should not be bent, distorted or otherwise altered to force them to fit. On completion, assembly work should be checked by a competent person with particular attention given to fastenings and connections. It is advisable to provide suitable covering for bolts and fittings which project into or adjoin public areas.

7.26 In order to prevent tampering with the framework, care should be taken to ensure that there is no unauthorised access beneath temporary structures.

Lifting operations

7.27 All items used for lifting should be suitable for their purpose. They should be stamped or marked with their safe working load or there should be a certificate giving the safe work load.

7.28 Where items are being passed up a structure e.g. by means of a line or a lift, no-one should be allowed in the area immediately below or adjacent to the load. Where lifting takes place without a winch this can be carried out from the ground over a pulley, gin wheel or block and tackle. Further information for those in charge of lifting operations is available in HSE Summary Sheet SS5, Suspended Cradles and Small Lifting Appliances.

7.29 Dismantling of structures should be carried out methodically, with items being handed or lowered down, not dropped or "bombed".

7.30 Lifting equipment, including wire ropes, winches, chain hoists, shackles, eye bolts, etc used to support any suspended equipment should comply with the requirements of the appropriate British Standard. A current certificate or record in the form required by the Lifting Plant and Equipment (Records of Tests and Examination) Regulations 1992, together with a copy of the register of inspection and maintenance of such equipment, should be held at the venue. Each hoist or winch should bear an approved stamp or mark to identify it with the apparatus referred to in the certificate.

7.31 Equipment and assemblies used for lifting should be stable and secure when in use.

7.32 Wire or man-made fibre ropes are safer than other types for lifting. However man-made fibre ropes may extend appreciably under load. A good guide is not to use a type with an extension of more than 5% under maximum permissible load.

7.33 It is advisable for drums or pulleys to have a diameter of at least 10 times that of a wire rope or 6 times that of a man-made fibre.

7.34 Powered winches should be operated only to raise or lower under power (ie should not allow a load to free fall). The design should ensure that no movement occurs unless power is applied (i.e. the braking mechanism is sufficient to hold the maximum load suspended and is automatically activated when the power is cut off).

7.35 The operation of a manual winch should not allow descent of the load by means of the brake. The load should be held between each stroke of the handle.

7.36 All hooks used for lifting should be fitted with a safety catch which should be in place during all lifting operations.

7.37 It is useful for the weight of the items to be lifted to be marked on the item itself or given in an accompanying certificate.

7.38 The person in charge of all lifting gear should inspect each item on delivery to the site and at the start of each day's work. Items which appear defective should not be used again unless a competent person (such as the supplier, manufacturer or insurer's engineer) certifies that they are in working condition.

7.39 Before lifting commences, it is good practice to test the lifting arrangements by raising slightly off the ground a proof load of 1.25 times the safe working load. However, the test will not be appropriate if the first lift is a full working load.

7.40 The loads to be carried by power-driven hoists or self-sustaining winches should be within the safe working load of the lifting equipment. In addition adequate provision should be made so that in the event of a failure, the load will not fall to the ground. One way of achieving this would be to use the hoists or winches in sufficient number so that in the event of one failing the others could safely sustain the load. Power-driven hoists with synchronising controls working together on the same structure ensure that an even lift is maintained.

Moving "flown" equipment

7.41 Any moving "flown" equipment used during or in connection with the concert should contain a device or method whereby any failure in the lifting system would not allow the load to fall. The inclusion of a control switch can allow isolation of the power and automatic braking of all motors for both upper and lower travel limits. The operator of the control switch requires a clear, uninterrupted view of all parts of the movable equipment. The operation of flown equipment should be tested before every performance prior to the admission of the public.

Note: "Flown" equipment includes any materials, hardware etc. attached to the superstructure of stands, stages etc.

7.42 Follow-spot operators are sometimes positioned on flown trusses or towers. Suitable safety harnesses and a means of escape, for example a rolled drop ladder, are needed for their safety.

STAGES

Loading

7.43 British Standard 6399 Part 1 recommends that stages should be designed for a live load of $7.5kN/m^2$ which takes into account the dynamic condition as well as static loads. The loading applies to all the areas associated with the stage including wings, the performance area, extension platforms, rostra and stage sets.

7.44 In certain limited circumstances, a lower stage loading than $7.5kN/m^2$ may be acceptable. The factors which would need to be considered include the number of people working on the stage, the movement which will take place and the absence of any risk of invasion of the stage by the audience. The loading, which should not be less than $5kN/m^2$, should be agreed by the licensing authority.

7.45 In addition, it is recommended that stages should be designed to carry a point load of 2.5kN over an area 50mm x 50mm without causing any damage to the floor and without causing excessive deflection of the floor panels (for example, deflection of more than 10mm relative to the adjoining panels).

7.46 The stage should be able to withstand horizontal pressure at its main floor level. In most circumstances, 10% of the live design load will be sufficient. If it is proposed to use a lower horizontal loading, and the stage could be subjected to high vibrations and rhythmic surge loads, the possibility of damage through harmonic response will need to be assessed.

7.47 Stages should be constructed in such a way as to remove any tripping or slipping hazards.

Dance platforms

7.48 Dance platforms, often used at "raves", should be designed to withstand a minimum live load of 5kN/m^2. Where it is expected that the number of people using the platform may be particularly great and where the forces they could impose may also be high, then the structure should be designed for a higher loading.

Access and egress

7.49 All stages over 1 metre in height should be provided with unobstructed access with clear vertical headroom, by means of ramps or stairways. The total access width should be at least 2 metres.

7.50 For large stages (eg over 40m^2) it is good practice to have at least two means of access/egress. It is also advisable to have a wider total access width (see also Chapters 12 to 15 for fire safety requirements).

7.51 The gradient of any ramp should be gradual enough to enable equipment to be moved safely . It is advisable for ramps to be no longer than 8 metres between horizontal landing areas. Landing areas should be at least 1 metre in length in the direction of travel and at least as wide as the access way/ramp.

7.52 The surface of any ramp or tread, particularly those which could become wet, should be covered with a slip-resistant material, for example, coarse sand on a painted surface, nailed down sanded roofing felt, step laths, carborundum or suitably secured sand coated paper.

7.53 Guidance on the minimum size of tread and maximum size of riser for stairways used for access is given in EC Harmonisation Document (HD 1004/92) on mobile access and working towers. The British Standards Institution intends to publish this document as a British Standard by the end of 1993.

7.54 Consideration should be given to the need for handrails at an appropriate height for stages, platforms and access ways. They will not be needed for the edge of the stage facing the audience but the edge should be clearly marked. Platforms over 1.8 metres in height should have either a clear space around them or a method of preventing objects falling onto people below.

7.55 If work is to take place on a completed structure at a height above stage platform level, an access platform will be needed to ensure that maintenance and adjustments can take place.

7.56 British Standard 1139 sets out requirements for handrails used in work areas only, such as stages and access platforms. This gives two criteria: a 0.3kN point load with a limiting deflection of 35mm; and a 1.25kN/m point load without breaking or deflecting more than 200mm at any point, both applied in a horizontal direction in the more severe location. Handrails used in areas to which the public have access and in any stage extension area to be used as a viewing platform should comply with the appropriate loading standards in British Standard 6399.

ADDITIONAL FACTORS FOR OUTDOOR STAGES

Wind loads

7.57 Stages at outdoor events should be designed according to the appropriate British Standard for wind loads. This is currently British Standard Code of Practice (CP) 3, Chapter V, Part 2 which makes provision for a lower wind load if the structure is to stand for two years or less.

7.58 Solid back walls should meet full wind load criteria, but those that consist of weatherwall, scrim, vinyl sheet or other similar flexible material may be discounted if it can be shown that:–

- they can be quickly removed without interfering with any "flown" production hardware or the stability of the remaining structure; or

- they are fitted with blow out panels arranged in such a way that there is no danger of injury to workers or the audience and the calculations take into account the effect of the remaining material; or

- they are attached by fixings which will fail at a predetermined wind pressure and there are satisfactory measures to prevent injury or damage from dislodged materials.

If any of these criteria apply, the initial drawings and calculations should be related to a given wind speed.

Roofs

7.59 Roofs should be designed to support the imposed loads as well as any self weight. Loading standards should be in accordance with British Standard 6399: Part 2.

7.60 The fixings of the covering should be capable of resisting any uplift forces caused by the maximum design wind load.

7.61 Calculations of the uplift forces along the eaves and gable, carried out at the design stage, should show whether the fixings for the roof coverings are able to withstand these forces. Some forms of roof covering experience severe vibration in high wind conditions and the vibration can shake loose certain types of fixing as well as cause early structural failure. Where these structures may be subjected to vibration the design should provide for these effects to be minimised.

TOWERS AND MASTS

7.62 It is desirable to construct towers and masts with a factor of safety against overturning of 3:1, i.e. so that the sum of all the forces tending to overturn the structure are less than one third of those forces keeping it upright. Examples of overturning forces are wind loads, or eccentric loading of the tower. Where the resistance to overturning is provided by the dead weight of the structure alone and this dead weight cannot be affected by an accidental removal or omission of components, the righting forces may be at least 1.5 of those that could overturn the structure. Where guying is used, care should be taken to ensure that the guys and their anchors do not cause an obstruction. All stakes or anchors should be located or covered so that they do not create a tripping hazard.

7.63 When calculating the eccentric loads on a tower, it should be assumed that all equipment and people are located at the most disadvantageous position. All other horizontal forces, for example caused by the use of heaving lines and ladders placed against the outside of the tower, need to be taken into account.

7.64 If towers are clad, they become more vulnerable to wind. Calculation of the wind load in any direction on towers and masts should take into account the effects of drag created by hoardings, banners or signs attached to any part of the structure.

7.65 It is preferable to lift loads up a tower within its plan area. Ladder or stair access, where provided, should also be located within the plan area.

7.66 Where vertical access ways through tower platforms are provided, they should not form an obstruction and it is advisable for them to be at least 700mm long by 600mm wide. There should be an intervening resting platform for every 6 metre ladder run (see also paragraph 7.53).

7.67 To prevent tampering, it is useful if towers are constructed in such a way that their structural sections cannot be removed without the use of specialised tools. The provision of a barrier with stewards, or boarding or cladding to a minimum height of 2.4 metres can stop the public climbing on the tower.

7.68 Masts should be constructed and sited so that unauthorised access is not possible.

7.69 Masts which are hinged should be secured against unauthorised interference by means of a locking mechanism to secure the hinge and, wherever possible, should have a secondary locking system.

TEMPORARY STANDS AND VIEWING PLATFORMS

Siting

7.70 The site should be carefully inspected before any assembly work starts in order to ensure that the load bearing capacity of the ground is adequate for the proposed occupied structure in all weather conditions. This may be done by digging trial holes or drilling under the inspection of a qualified engineer. The site should also allow suitable access and egress for the audience both from the public highway and adjacent facilities.

Assembly

7.71 The assembly of temporary stands and viewing platforms should be carried out in accordance with plans and specifications drawn up by a competent engineer. British Standard Code of Practice (CP) 3: Chapter V: Part 2: 1972 sets out standards to which canopies and covers on stands should be designed. The event safety co-ordinator should monitor the erection of these structures and ensure that safe working practices are followed.

Seating

7.72 All seats should be securely fixed in position. The Home Office/The Scottish Office "Guide to Fire Precautions in Existing Places of Entertainment and Like Premises" recommends that to enable people to move freely between rows of seats, there should be an unobstructed space of at least 305mm between the back of one seat and the front of the seat immediately behind.

7.73 The Home Office/The Scottish Office "Guide to Safety at Sports Grounds" recommends that the number of seats in a row should not normally exceed:-

- 14 where there is a gangway at one end only; and

- 28 where there is a gangway at both ends.

It also recommends that seats and gangways should be so positioned as to provide ready access to exits and to ensure that normally nobody has to travel more than 30 metres to reach the exit from the viewing area of a stand. It is suggested that these standards are appropriate for temporary stands at pop concerts.

7.74 Stewards should be aware of the seating capacity of each stand and ensure that they are not overcrowded.

Means of escape and fire safety

7.75 Temporary stands should be constructed to include a minimum of two readily accessible alternative exit routes which should be adequately indicated by exit and directional exit signs.

7.76 If an entertainment extends beyond daylight hours, temporary stands should be provided with normal and emergency escape lighting.

7.77 The structure of temporary stands should have adequate resistance to the rapid spread of fire, heat and smoke as should any fixtures and fittings. Litter and combustible refuse should not be stored or allowed to accumulate beneath a temporary stand.

7.78 Concessions and sanitary conveniences should not normally be situated on or attached to a temporary stand. If this is unavoidable, any concessions etc. should be separated from the viewing area and exit routes by fire-resisting construction, and located so as not to obstruct the escape routes. Additionally, any structures forming facilities for concessions should not put any unacceptable loads or forces on the stand i.e. where necessary, the design of the stand should allow for any such loadings, and calculations should take this into account.

NOTES/AMENDMENTS

MARQUEES AND LARGE TENTS

Erecting marquees and tents

8.1 Marquees and large tents should be capable of withstanding wind forces and loadings particularly those caused by bad weather conditions. For instance, in heavy rain or if the ground is flooded there is a possibility of ground anchorage being loosened or undermined. Other considerations include:-

- in strong winds, the regular tightening of guy ropes and the need to ensure that pegs are firmly anchored; and

- in wet weather, the slackening of guy ropes and, in extreme conditions, the digging of drainage ditches.

8.2 Marquees should be erected by competent persons with all supporting poles, frames, guys, stakes, anchors, fastenings, etc. checked regularly on site. The structural integrity of marquees is the responsibility of either the owner of the marquee or other nominated competent persons and should be monitored by the event safety co-ordinator.

8.3 Exit routes from marquees may be over uneven ground, temporary flooring, duckboards, ramps, etc. These factors should be taken into account to ensure that there are safe access and egress routes.

8.4 If it is intended that a load should be hung from a marquee, the marquee supplier should be asked to confirm that the structure will stand such a load. The licensing authority is likely to request details of calculations for larger weights (e.g. over 100kg).

8.5 Siting pedestrian routes away from marquees avoids the tripping hazard of guy ropes or stakes. If a large number of people are expected to pass close to a marquee, marking or suitably covering guy ropes and stakes is advisable. Wherever practicable, vehicular routes should avoid the areas around marquees. Where this is not possible, the marquee should be protected e.g. by the erection of barriers.

Emergency and fire considerations

8.6 Licensing authorities will require all membranes and fabrics used in a marquee to be flame retardant. Newly manufactured materials should be of inherently flame-retarded fabric or durably flame-retarded fabric when tested to British Standard 5438, Tests 2a and 2b with a ten-second flame application time in each case. The method of test described in British Standard 7157 is also acceptable. Existing materials and structures manufactured to British Standard 3120 only remain acceptable until 31 December 1995. Solid sheet materials should be of not less than Class 1 surface spread of flame in accordance with British Standard 476: Part 7. Materials should be free of flaming molten droplet characteristics and should not readily support combustion.

8.7 The licensing authority will generally require the event organiser to provide a certificate or other evidence from a body of recognised standing to show compliance with the provisions of paragraph 8.6 but even if no licence is required for the event, it would be good practice for the event organiser to obtain such a certificate.

8.8 Marquees or tented complexes should normally be spaced about 6 metres apart to prevent the spread of fire and allow access by the emergency services. Tented complexes, i.e. an interconnected group of tents erected for related purposes, should be laid out in such a way that fire appliances can reach to within 50 metres of any part of the complex.

8.9 Tented structures should be equipped with :–

- an adequate number of emergency exits of a suitable size;

- appropriate means for giving warning in case of fire;

- normal and emergency escape lighting and emergency exit signs; and

- fire-fighting equipment.

In practice, a marquee will generally have emergency exits appropriate to its size and exit signs. The organiser or manager will need to provide a means for giving warning in the event of fire, lighting, fire-fighting equipment and any additional signs which may be needed because of the internal arrangements of the marquee.

8.10 The seating arrangements described in paragraphs 7.72 and 7.73 for temporary stands and viewing platforms are equally appropriate for seating within tented structures.

8.11 Organisers should be aware of the need to site any special effects such as firework displays well away from marquees and large tents.

8.12 Exits should be sufficient for the number of occupants in relation to their width, number and siting. Normally no exit should be less than 1 metre wide.

8.13 Exits should be clearly indicated and if they consist of wall flaps they should be of a quick release design, clearly defined at the edges and so arranged as to be easily and immediately opened from the inside. Conditions of licence may call for fixed door and frame exits consisting of conventional outward opening doors fitted with suitable emergency fastenings. Among the factors which may make fixed door and frame exits necessary are:–

- a large floor area and large numbers of people;

- tiered seating, the presence of tables and use as a restaurant;

- the presence of services, i.e. LPG, portable heating and cooking arrangements;

- the presence of combustible materials;

- the presence of people with disabilities; and

- the fact that alcohol is sold.

8.14 There should be at least two exits from a marquee, and all exits should be distributed evenly around the marquee so that genuine alternative routes are available.

8.15 Although the general principle is that no-one should have to travel more than 18 metres to reach an exit, this is not inflexible as a number of factors may influence the situation. For instance, a high risk of fire spread may require a shorter travel distance whilst an effective fire safety policy, sufficient trained stewards and suitable signposting of exit routes may permit longer travel distances.

8.16 It should be noted that where a temporary ramp or temporary stairway forms part of the means of escape an additional 0.25 metres should be added to the calculation of travel distance for every 1 metre of the ramp or stairway. Thus if the actual distance to a final exit is 18 metres, of which 10 metres is a temporary stairway, the distance of travel would be regarded as 20.5 metres.

8.17 Cutting all long grass around a marquee before it is erected and removing the cuttings helps to prevent the risk of fire.

Provision of fire fighting equipment

8.18 Chapter 13 describes the types of fire extinguisher which are available and their uses. Suitable extinguishers should be provided to deal with individual risks e.g. electrical, flammable gases, etc. and the principle concerning the scale of issue of water extinguishers set out in paragraph 13.13 is equally appropriate to tented structures.

Floor coverings

8.19 Where flooring is used in marquees or large tents it should meet the appropriate British Standard in respect of reaction to fire. The most appropriate fire test is British Standard 4790 Method of Determination of the Effects of a Small Source of Ignition on Textile Floor Coverings (hot metal nut method). This test is for all types of covering whether loose laid, fully adhered or used with underlay, and flooring should comply with the low radius of effect of ignition found in Table 1 of British Standard 5287 Specification for the Assessment and Labelling of Textile Floor coverings tested to British Standard 4790. Another test is British Standard 6307 Method for the Determination of the Effects of a Small Source of Ignition on Textile Floor Coverings (methenamine tablet test). British Standard 4790 is supplemented by British Standard 6307 which is a dual BSI/ISO standard.

8.20 If the organiser is in any doubt, advice should be sought from the licensing authority.

NOTES/AMENDMENTS

ELECTRICAL SYSTEMS

Introduction

9.1 Electrical installations at concert sites, particularly at large outdoor events, can be complicated and extensive. If not installed and managed correctly, serious injury to employees and/or members of the public can occur. For instance, incompatible equipment and incorrect connections may cause electric shocks and overloading of circuits can lead to lighting failure or result in a fire.

9.2 All electrical installations and equipment must comply with the general requirements of the Electricity at Work Regulations 1989. This can best be achieved by ensuring that the installation is installed, tested and maintained in accordance with the latest edition of the Institution of Electrical Engineers' "Regulations for Electrical Installations" (The IEE Wiring Regulations) which now also form British Standard 7671, "The Requirements for Wiring Installations". Other useful references are HSE Guidance Note GS50 "Electrical Safety at places of entertainment" and HSE booklet IND (G) 102L "Electrical Safety for Entertainers".

Assessment

9.3 The event organiser will need to assess the electrical requirements for the following uses:-

- sited stage audio systems;

- stage and effect lighting;

- normal and emergency lighting circuits;

- power supply for hoists, portable tools, etc; and

- miscellaneous power supplies including back-up supplies for heaters, catering equipment, electric motors, incident control centre etc.

The organiser will then need to decide whether existing provisions are satisfactory, and if they are not, provide suitable additional facilities.

9.4 Additionally the event organiser, in liaison with the safety co-ordinator and electrical contractor, should assess whether the electricity supply for the venue is compatible with the equipment to be used. This may be a particular problem where the concert features performers from abroad.

9.5 The designs and types of electrical connectors need careful consideration. Electric guitars and other low voltage equipment require suitable low voltage connectors. Those responsible for setting up performers' electrical equipment should check that all connections fit and are compatible. Equipment which uses alternating current (AC) and that which uses extra low voltage battery supplies needs to be clearly identified.

Installation

9.6   All electrical equipment should be installed, so far as is reasonably practicable, so that is cannot be interfered with by the public or unauthorised employees.

9.7   Wherever possible, sufficient fixed socket outlets should be provided within the stage area to avoid the use of flexible extension leads and multi-socket outlets. Fixed socket outlets can be either permanent or properly mounted distribution boards. It is also advisable for equipment to be located within 2 metres of a fixed socket outlet to prevent long trailing leads.

9.8   All equipment which may be exposed to weather should be suitably constructed and protected.

9.9   Where electricity has to be used in areas of higher risk, e.g. wet conditions, or where there are trailing sockets not designed to make and break on load, the guidance contained in British Standard 4343 "Specification for industrial plugs, socket outlets and couplers, etc" should be followed.

9.10   On completion of any permanent electrical installation, an electrical certificate in the form prescribed in the Institution of Electrical Engineers Wiring regulations, signed by a competent person, is likely to be required by the licensing authority. For temporary installations a similar certificate appropriate to the nature of the installation may be needed.

Cabling

9.11   Wherever possible, cables should be routed or buried so that they will not cause a tripping hazard or be crushed by vehicular traffic. Cables carrying hazardous voltages, e.g. those which could cause an electric shock if damaged, should also be protected against contact with sharp edges or crushing by heavy loads. This can be achieved by providing additional resilient sheathing or metallic armouring or, as an alternative, the cable can be routed overhead.

9.12   Cables installed underground to prevent a tripping hazard need only be buried just under the surface. Power cables however should be armoured and buried at an adequate depth for the foreseeable hazards. For example, under a pedestrian access-way, turf-depth would be adequate, but within the audience area, the cable should be below the level reached by tent pegs, posts for umbrellas etc. Across vehicle access-ways, the depth will depend on the weight of vehicles. For cars and light service traffic, armoured power cables should be buried a minimum of 200mm below the surface. However, for heavier commercial vehicles, e.g. large generators, transportable staging etc, the cable may need to be deeper, or beneath a protective metal plate. Where the power cable cannot be buried, e.g. across a metalled road, it should be protected by suitable metal plate.

9.13 Two documents developed in conjunction with the electricity supply industry provide guidance for the avoidance of danger from overhead lines and underground cables. These are:–

- "Avoidance of Danger from Overhead Electricity Lines" (GS6); and

- "Avoidance of Danger from Underground Services" (HS(G)47).

9.14 All temporary overhead electrical wiring should be securely fixed in position or supported by a catenary wire which is out of reach of the public and arranged so that no undue strain is placed upon the conductors or insulation of the cable. Wherever possible, traffic and cable routes should be segregated. If this is not possible, a cable height of 5.8 metres is advisable to cater for the highest likely vehicle. The catenary wire should be earthed.

9.15 All power distribution cables should conform to the relevant British Standard and be sized in accordance with the appropriate table in the IEE Wiring Regulations, current at the time of installation. Cables used on stage or for stage equipment should be flexible, rubber or PVC-insulated and sheathed as specified in British Standard 6007 or be of equivalent quality.

Note: Reference should also be made to Part 7 of British Standard 5550 in regard to the Code of Practice for distribution of AC electricity for location lighting.

Access to control systems

9.16 A clear working space is required to facilitate access to:-

- control switches and equipment;

- amplification equipment;

- special effects equipment;

- follow spots; and

- high voltage discharge lighting, e.g. neon.

9.17 The main controls should be clearly identified and their location notified to the police and fire service. All switchgear should be protected to prevent access and tampering by unauthorised persons. Where switchgear is installed in a locked enclosure, specific keyholders should be given responsibility for operating the equipment to comply safely with any request by the emergency services, e.g. to electrically isolate the stage whilst leaving audience lighting operating.

Electricity to the stage area and effect lighting

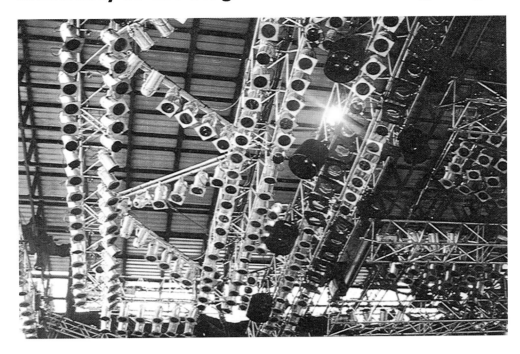

9.18 The electricity supply to the stage should be controlled by a switch or switches, installed in a position readily accessible to authorised persons in the stage area. The switches should be able to isolate the circuit on both poles in the case of single phase supply or on all live poles in the case of polyphase (3 phase) supply. Where the power to the stage is provided by on-site generators, 4 pole (i.e. three phase + neutral) isolation should be installed.

9.19 In order to prevent contact with scenery or other combustible material, all lamps, lighting equipment and any other apparatus likely to reach a high temperature should be suitably guarded.

9.20 Equipment to light the stage should not be suspended over the parts of the venue to which the public have access unless the conditions set out in paragraph 9.21 are met. In some circumstances, a certificate from a qualified structural engineer will be needed. This should state that the roof structure, suspension points and equipment have been inspected and that the loadings and components are installed to a safe standard.

9.21 Any lantern or other suspended lighting apparatus should have a suitable safety chain or safety wire fitted. The weight of any flown lighting equipment should not exceed the safe working load of securing points. No flown or suspended equipment, including lighting bars and amplification equipment, should rely solely on one suspension cable, clamp or bolt. Each means of suspension should be secured to independent fixing points on the flown equipment and the structure.

9.22 Heavy pendant fittings or apparatus should, unless directly fixed to the permanent infrastructure, be provided with at least two non-combustible means of suspension. The electric power cable is not suitable to carry any part of the weight of the apparatus, unless it has been designed for that application, in which case only one other means of suspension need be provided.

Note: Suspension ropes (both primary and secondary) should normally be of flexible steel or metal chain. Webbed strapping may be acceptable as one of the suspensions provided it is fire resistant and proof of its fire-resisting properties and safe working load are available.

9.23 Scaffolding, metal frameworks, bars and booms on which electrical equipment is fixed should be efficiently earthed.

Normal lighting circuits

9.24 All parts of the venue should, if intended for use in the absence of adequate daylight, be provided with suitable levels of artificial lighting.

9.25 Areas to be lit include first aid, welfare and information marquees, pedestrian access to car parks, car parking areas and access routes to public highways. The provision of lighting will depend on individual sites and the existing lighting system. It is important to protect the system from interference by unauthorised persons.

9.26 All venues should be provided with appropriate exit and directional signs indicating the escape routes. Such signs should, where appropriate, be lit by means of the normal and the emergency escape lighting (see paragraph 9.31).

9.27 At venues where exit and directional signs may need to be viewed from afar, particular attention needs to be given to the quality and intensity of lighting.

Emergency lighting circuits

9.28 In addition to the normal lighting arrangements, all parts of the venue accessible to the public and all exit routes, if they may be used in the absence of adequate daylight, require a system of emergency lighting supplied from a source of electricity independent of the normal lighting. If a generator is used, it may be necessary for this to be earthed or bonded to the exposed conductive parts of the other electrical systems on site. The emergency lighting should be of a maintained type (continuously illuminated). Emergency lighting arrangements should be in accordance with British Standard 5266 (see paragraph 9.31).

Note: In the case of open air venues, all exit routes, areas presenting a hazard (e.g. pits, holes, trenches, ditches etc.), areas containing emergency equipment, and emergency signs and/or notices should be provided with emergency lighting to at least the minimum standard recommended in British Standard 5266.

9.29 Any source of supply used for providing emergency lighting should be capable of maintaining the full lighting load for not less than 3 hours in the event of failure of the normal supply. It is important to keep any battery used for this purpose in a fully charged condition whenever the venue is in use.

9.30 Where the alternative supply is by means of a generator this should be kept running throughout the time of the concert. A fuel supply capable of maintaining the full lighting load for not less than 3 hours is needed in the event of failure of the mains supply. It may be necessary to provide access to the generator for refuelling.

Lighting levels for means of escape

9.31 All parts of the venue to which the public have access should be provided with normal and emergency lighting capable of giving sufficient illumination for people to leave safely. For stairways, corridors, exit doorways, gates etc, the average illumination level should be 20 lux and the minimum should be 5 lux.

Management of lighting circuits

9.32 The control for operating the normal and the emergency lighting systems should not be accessible to unauthorised persons.

9.33 The normal and emergency lighting systems should be installed so that a fault or accident arising to one system cannot jeopardize the other.

9.34 At larger events, the normal and emergency lighting systems are usually split into a number of separate circuits. Suitable provision should be made to enable repairs to be undertaken if part of these lighting systems fails.

9.35 If the lighting systems are not split in this way, and either of the systems fail in circumstances where the natural source of lighting is not sufficient, the concert may have to be terminated (see Chapter 16 for emergency procedures).

9.36 Dimming equipment should be sited in an approved position and be under the control of a competent person whilst the public are present.

Generators and transformers

9.37 Particular care is needed where generators are used to supply power. Detailed advice and information is given in the HSE guidance note GS(50) – Electrical Safety at Places of Entertainment and the HSE booklet – Electrical Safety for Entertainers.

9.38 Where applicable, transformers should comply with the requirements of the relevant British Standards and be installed in accordance with the IEE Wiring Regulations current at the time of installation.

9.39 British Standard 7430, Code of Practice for Earthing, gives guidance on the earthing of mobile generators for outdoor events.

RCDs and other equipment

9.40 Each item of apparatus, e.g. smoke-producing machines (see Chapter 10), follow spots etc, should be provided with a local means of isolation which may be a plug and socket of suitable rating appropriately placed for ready operation.

9.41 Colour filters for effects lighting etc should comply with the flammability requirements of British Standard 3944, Specification for Colour Filters for Theatre Lighting and other purposes.

9.42 Any electrical equipment used in association with hand held devices, e.g. microphones, should be protected by a miniature circuit breaker and also a residual current device (RCD) having a 30 mA tripping current and installed on a distribution board (not a plug-in type). It is also advisable for an RCD to be provided for dry ice machines. RCDs should be tested when installed, operated by the test button before the event starts and fully tested every 6 months by a competent operator. The normal and emergency lighting circuits should not be affected by the operation of an RCD.

9.43 If any electrical equipment is not isolated and locked off whilst the public are present, then a competent person should be present to operate the relevant equipment during an emergency. Since the required action could vary from operating a light switch to operating a computer controlled console, the competent person needs to understand the system over which they have control. It may be necessary, particularly at large outdoor concerts, for there to be more than one competent person, i.e. one present on the stage and another elsewhere in the venue. It is also important that there is an effective means of communication between the electricians and the manager.

9.44 At small venues with a fixed electrical installation and no temporary installation, other than the plug-in equipment used by the performers, the event organiser or manager may decide that it is only necessary to have an electrician "on-call".

9.45 All electrically powered equipment should be maintained to ensure compliance with the Electricity at Work Regulations.

NOTES/AMENDMENTS

Chapter 10

SPECIAL EFFECTS AND PYROTECHNICS

Introduction

10.1   This chapter gives guidance on the use of special effects and pyrotechnics in order to safeguard the public, performers and employees from injury.

Lasers

10.2   Laser displays are widely used at concerts and other entertainments. HSE Guidance Note PM19 "Use of Lasers for Display Purposes" gives advice on the installation and operation of lasers and sets out ways to safeguard the audience and employees at the venue. Those lasers which can cause harmful effects, because they are often able to exceed the maximum permissible exposure (MPE) limits in a few micro seconds, need to be carefully managed.

Note: This document is being revised and will shortly be published as HS(G)95 "Guidance on the Radiation Safety of Lasers used for Display Purposes".

10.3   The British Standard (BS EN 60825, Radiation Safety of Laser Products, Equipment Classification, Requirements and Users' Guide) groups lasers into four main classes. Class 1 lasers are inherently safe but all other lasers can cause eye damage under certain conditions. Class 4 lasers will cause eye damage if viewed directly.

10.4   No one carrying out tests, attending rehearsals or the actual performance should be able to view laser radiation which exceeds the applicable MPE. If exposure is only likely to be inadvertent, the applicable MPE may be based upon an exposure time-base that "assumes" competent eye aversion responses.

10.5   Designers and suppliers of laser displays and products need to be aware that eye safety for accidental direct viewing of Class 2 or 3A lasers relies upon human aversion responses, e.g. blinking, and that such reflexes could be affected by alcohol or drugs and thus reduce the margin of safety.

10.6   British Standard EN 60825 requires that for installations where Class 3B and Class 4 lasers are operated, a laser safety officer, knowledgeable in the evaluation and control of laser hazards, should be appointed. It is the laser safety officer's task to review the precautions necessary to operate the laser safely, and to advise on appropriate controls.

10.7   Each laser supplier or operator of the laser display should have access to an employee or an external consultant who is capable of performing the duties of a laser safety officer. This person should advise on the safety aspects of any new installation, examine the equipment itself, its incorporated safety devices and systems, and ensure that handover documents are adequate.

10.8   The handover document should contain a detailed specification of the intended scope of the display and the operator should not deviate from that specification. This document should be specific to the venue where the laser display is to occur and should include a drawing of the laser display area in both plan and elevation. The positions of laser sources, mirrors and target areas should be clearly marked, along with the relevant distances and dimensions. The licensing authority will normally ask to see a copy of the handover documents.

10.9 At open air displays security is particularly important to prevent any interference with the installation. In addition, factors such as unintended reflections from surrounding structures, nearby traffic movements and adverse weather conditions will need to be considered.

"Strobe" lights

10.10 Organisers should carefully consider whether to use strobe lights during events as they have been known to induce epilepsy. When they are used, the event organiser should arrange for a warning to be given, for example at the entrance to the event or in the programme. Flicker sensitive epilepsy is a condition which may be triggered by a number of factors, including television. Although this condition is rare, if an episode is triggered, there is a high risk that the flicker-sensitive individual will most likely experience a full seizure.

10.11 If strobe lights are used, it is recommended that flicker rates are kept at or below 4 flashes per second (as then only 5% of the flicker-sensitive population will be at risk of an attack). This flicker rate only applies to the overall output of any group of lights in direct view but where more than one strobe light is used, the flashes should be synchronised.

Ultraviolet light

10.12 Ultraviolet light is sometimes used at pop concerts to produce a fluorescent effect on clothing or stage scenery.

10.13 Great care needs to be taken to ensure that lamps are used correctly in order to restrict exposure to ultraviolet radiation and in particular to UVB radiation. In order to remove UVB radiation, some lamps have a double skin whereas other manufacturers provide lamp housings which have separate filters. Lamps should not be used if the outer skin is broken or if the housing filter is not in place. Operators need to know the emission characteristics of the lamps in relation to the required spectral distribution. When replacing lamps or other components which could affect the radiation output, it is important that the manufacturers' advice is followed.

10.14 There may be significant exposure to performers or backstage staff during rehearsals or in the preparation of the set. These risks can be controlled by limiting the length of time people are exposed or increasing the distance from the source, in accordance with the manufacturers' instructions.

10.15 Some people may have an abnormally increased sensitivity to the effects of ultraviolet light on the skin. This can either be because of one of a number of uncommon medical conditions, or because they are taking a drug. Such sensitization may result in an exaggerated sunburn reaction or in other skin changes. Any worker who develops an abnormal condition affecting the light exposed areas of the body may have become photosensitized. Further occupational exposure to ultraviolet light should be stopped and the person advised to seek medical help.

Pyrotechnics

10.16 "Pyrotechnics", for the purpose of this guidance, covers a wide variety of explosive devices, including fireworks, as defined in British Standard 7114: Part 1 and devices which are not subject to the British Standard including theatrical and film effects, flares, and signal rockets.

10.17 In order to ensure that effective liaison takes place, the event organiser should ensure that the manager is given the name of the individual who will be responsible for any pyrotechnics at the event.

Legislation

10.18 The Explosives Acts 1875 and 1923 govern the storage of explosive substances while the use of explosives is covered by other legislation, including the general provisions of the Health and Safety at Work Act 1974.

10.19 The Control of Explosives Regulations, which came into force on 1 November 1991, introduced a new certificate (an explosives certificate) to authorise the acquisition and keeping of certain explosives. A leaflet and guidance about the new regulations are available from HSE. An explosives certificate will not be required for fireworks and some other explosives used for pyrotechnic effects. However, the event organiser should discuss any proposal to keep explosives with the local authority responsible for registration or licensing under the Explosives Act 1875, who will be able to advise whether an explosives certificate is needed.

Firework displays

10.20 Under Regulation 10(2) of the Control of Explosives Regulations 1991, up to 5kg of fireworks may be kept for private use (i.e. not for sale) indefinitely, and an unlimited quantity may be kept for private use for up to 14 days before they are used. The fireworks must be kept in a safe place with all due precautions for public safety.

10.21 Otherwise, pyrotechnics must be kept in a store licensed by the local authority, in local authority registered premises, or in a licensed factory or magazine. Full details of these requirements may be obtained from local authority trading standards officers. The local authority inspects premises annually to check on quantities kept and to ensure that storage requirements are adequate.

10.22 Firework displays should be organised in accordance with the recommendations in the code "Safer displays: a guide to firework safety" issued by the Consumer Safety Unit of the Department of Trade and Industry.

Use of pyrotechnics

10.23 Pyrotechnics should only be used for the event if approved by the licensing authority. A licence is required from HSE for the importation of pyrotechnics into the United Kingdom.

10.24 All pyrotechnics should be used strictly in accordance with manufacturers' and suppliers' instructions and recommendations.

10.25 Pyrotechnics should be the responsibility of a person competent to handle them, who has been adequately trained, instructed or made aware of the correct method of control and operation, and of any special safety methods required. This person should also be satisfied that anyone else who may need to use pyrotechnics during the entertainment has also been adequately instructed.

Safety factors

10.26 The firing device should be electrically and mechanically safe and maintained in good condition.

10.27 Pyrotechnic devices should always be fired using a properly designed and constructed firing box. This may be powered from mains electricity or from a suitable battery and should be capable of being isolated by means of a key operated isolation switch. The key should be in the possession of the operator firing the device. Electrically operated devices should be capable of being isolated from their firing supply by the complete disconnection of the supply cable.

10.28 The electrical supply for firing boxes should be constant, and not subject to fluctuation, e.g. reduced voltage through use of dimmers.

10.29 Storage receptacles for pyrotechnic devices should be of substantial construction with a notice bearing the words "Danger – No Smoking – No Naked Flame" displayed on the outside of the lid.

10.30 All receptacles and enclosures used for storing pyrotechnics should be kept locked except when access is needed. Enclosures should have a "no smoking" notice fixed on the external face of the door. The person responsible for security, keeping of records and for storing the materials safely should keep the keys. If types of explosives are kept which require an explosives certificate under the Control of Explosives Regulations 1991, additional security measures, such as patrols or alarms, may be needed.

Smoke and vapour effects

10.31 There are two ways of producing smoke and vapour for special effects:–

- solid carbon dioxide (dry ice) or liquid nitrogen fog machines; and
- fluid-based smoke machines.

10.32 To achieve a mist-like effect on stage, solid carbon dioxide (dry ice) is immersed in hot water or steam so that white clouds are produced which drift along the stage at floor level. The resulting mist is frequently directed by the use of ducting and fans.

10.33 Dry ice should be handled only with imperforate gloves having good thermal insulation, as momentary skin contact causes serious frostbite and blisters. Medium term storage is possible in containers with good insulation, but these should be vented and sited in well-ventilated areas. As small pieces of dry ice vaporize rapidly, it is advisable not to break up blocks of dry ice until immediately before use.

10.34 Liquid nitrogen is increasingly being used to create vapour effects. Special care should be taken when handling liquid nitrogen as it is extremely cold and causes severe frostbite on contact with the skin. It is therefore advisable to wear long insulated gloves and face visors to ensure that no skin is left uncovered in order to avoid hazards from splashing. Liquid nitrogen should be stored in the container in which it is supplied.

10.35 It is useful to consult the suppliers for further information on storage, handling and use.

10.36 Carbon dioxide and nitrogen gases are asphyxiants and high concentrations can present dangers to the audience, performers and stage staff. Good ventilation is therefore necessary. Particular care needs to be taken at indoor venues which have under-stage basement workshops/storage areas as the vapour may flow into these areas through openings and crevices putting people at risk.

10.37 Following initial generation, the vapours become invisible and the concentration of gas may be difficult to determine. If, during any test prior to its use at a performance, there is any doubt about the concentration present, it is recommended that expert advice be sought to monitor the oxygen and carbon dioxide levels before the equipment is used for a performance.

10.38 Smoke machines are mainly used to enhance lighting and special effects and should only be operated in accordance with the manufacturer's written instructions.

Use of smoke or fog machine

10.39 Where a smoke or fog machine is used there needs to be adequate ventilation of the affected area. The amount of smoke/vapour in the areas to which the public are admitted should be limited to the minimum necessary for the desired effect.

10.40 Fans can be used, where necessary, to direct the smoke/vapour into the desired area in order to prevent clouding at the point of discharge and possible overspill into other parts of the venue. Smoke or vapour should not be discharged or drift into exits, exitways, stairways, escape routes, etc. or be allowed to obscure exit signs or fire protection equipment.

Note: Before approving the use of a smoke or vapour effect, the licensing authority/fire authority will consider the presence of any automatic fire detection or fire sensor system installed in the venue.

10.41 The machine should be in a fixed position, adequately protected against unauthorised interference, and staffed or be readily accessible to a competent operator at all times when it is being used. The smoke/vapour outlets should also be within sight of the operator at all times.

10.42 The licensing authority will normally require the event organiser to produce documentary evidence of the non-toxicity and non-flammability of the smoke unless the type of equipment is in common use.

NOTES/AMENDMENTS

Chapter 11

SOUND AND NOISE

Introduction

11.1 Excessive sound levels can create a risk to hearing, both for those working at an event and the audience. It can also create a noise nuisance outside the venue. Effective *monitoring* and effective *control* of noise levels is therefore needed both in rehearsal and during the event.

11.2 Generally speaking, any very loud sound, including music, can damage hearing if people are exposed to it for lengthy periods, for example if they work every day in noisy surroundings. As the sound level increases, there will be a much quicker effect in damaging hearing. At extremely high levels, there may be a risk of immediate damage.

11.3 Most members of the audience will not attend events regularly enough to suffer serious hearing damage solely as a result of going to pop concerts. However, the louder events can contribute significantly to the overall sound and noise exposures that members of the audience may receive in other leisure activities and at work, so increasing the overall risk to their hearing.

11.4 There are legal obligations (under the HSW Act and the Noise at Work Regulations 1989) on those who organise events, for the protection both of workers and the audience from noise. The Management of Health & Safety at Work Regulations 1992 also apply .

11.5 The Noise Council have produced a draft code for public comment which gives guidance and possible measures for minimising environmental noise in the surrounding area.

Levels of exposure

11.6 There is information at Appendix 3 about the units used for measuring noise.

Workers

11.7 The Noise at Work Regulations 1989 protect workers. They set out action which must be taken when various Action Levels of exposure are reached.

If exposure is likely to reach 85dB(A) Action Level employers need to:-

- ensure that a noise assessment is made by a competent person (this is also needed if sound pressure peaks might reach 140 dB);

- provide workers with information and training; and

- provide ear protectors for all workers who ask for them.

If exposure is likely to reach 90dB(A) Action Level or a peak sound pressure of 140 dB employers also need to:-

- reduce exposures as far as reasonably practicable by reducing sound levels or the need to work for long periods in noisy areas;

- provide ear protectors to all workers and ensure that they are used. The regulations also require the workers to use them; and

- mark ear protection zones and make sure that everyone who goes into them uses ear protectors. These may well include the entrances to the front barrier area and the areas surrounding delay tower loudspeakers.

11.8 Detailed advice on the regulations is given in HSE Noise Guides 1 and 2 (published in a single volume) and HSE Noise Guides 3 to 8 (published in a single volume). Free leaflets on the regulations are available from HSE.

Audience

11.9 There is no legislation setting noise limits for audience exposure to loud sound. But there are general requirements in the Act which have the effect that audiences need to be protected against risk to their hearing.

11.10 It is undesirable for the Event Equivalent Continuous Sound Level (Event Leq) in audience areas to exceed 107dB(A), or for the peak sound pressure to exceed 140dB. The precise description of these levels and the conventions for measuring them are given in Appendix 3. It is recommended that audiences should not be allowed within 3 metres of any speaker at outdoor events. If the Event Leq is likely to exceed 96dB (A) it is good practice to warn audiences about the risk to hearing in advance publicity, e.g. in programme advertising, notices at entry points or on tickets.

CONTROLLING AND MONITORING SOUND LEVELS

Assessment

11.11 If sound levels are to be effectively managed, efficient arrangements will be needed for a pre-event assessment which includes the sound levels likely to be produced, and for monitoring and controlling the levels during the event, sound checks and rehearsals. Assessment of audience and external noise nuisance levels is usually best combined with the noise assessment for workers required by the Noise at Work Regulations.

It is recommended that this assessment includes establishing whether:-

- the sound levels likely in the audience area are within the values recommended in paragraph 11.10;

- the sound levels are likely to reach the value at which warnings are recommended in 11. 10;

- any of the workers' noise exposures are likely to reach any of the Action Levels set out in the Noise at Work Regulations;

- there are areas within the perimeter which should be marked as ear protection zones; and

- the arrangements for monitoring and control during the event will be adequate.

11.12 The assessment should include sound levels inside and outside the venue. A good pre-event assessment will take into account the position of the loudspeakers and the likely density and distribution of the audience. The possibility that sound transmitted through the ground and staging, particularly bass and sub-bass, could affect the integrity of structures should also be taken into account. It is also important to assess public address systems which may be used to convey safety information not only for loudness but also for audibility and intelligibility.

Controlling sound levels

11.13 The main general need is for a well designed sound system which minimises the variation in loudness throughout the audience area. This helps to avoid the need for high sound levels at the front in order to obtain an acceptable level at the rear. A well designed system can also help to avoid neighbourhood noise nuisance.

11.14 Measures to control worker exposure might include:-

- shielding work areas;

- reducing the length of time they need to spend in noisy areas; and

- reducing the music level during rehearsals.

11.15 Where workers are still likely to receive exposures above the Action Levels in the Noise at Work Regulations, ear protectors will be needed. If it is likely that workers will not have ear protectors with them, it is best for ear plug dispensers to be provided near to ear protection zones or other suitable points. If dispensers are used they should be checked and replenished from time to time.

11.16 Sound levels often tend to rise during an event, for example to maintain impact or to emphasise leading performers who appear at the end of the programme. Where this is planned to happen, the level for earlier items should be set to allow for the increase without exceeding any overall limit.

11.17 If control of the sound system is to be transferred to another engineer during the event all the engineers involved need to be informed about the sound level monitoring and control system and how it works.

Monitoring sound levels

11.18 It is necessary to monitor the sound level in order to see that it is being properly controlled during sound checks, rehearsals and the event itself. It is also often advisable to have a single system which is capable of monitoring inside and outside the event.

11.19 Monitoring can be continuous or for a series of short periods e.g. up to 15 minutes each time. Sound levels for the audience are best checked at head height in the loudest part of the audience area, usually close to the front of stage barrier. If the sound level is measured elsewhere (e.g. at the mixer desk) a correction needs to be estimated during the initial assessment and applied to allow for the difference between that measurement point and the loudest area.

11.20 Particularly during the event, those involved in monitoring and controlling sound levels need to be able to maintain a dialogue. If monitoring indicates that the sound level in the audience area is likely to be too high, the sound engineer needs to be advised to adjust the system immediately.

NOTES/AMENDMENTS

PART III

FIRE SAFETY AND EMERGENCY

PROCEDURES

Chapter 12: # MEANS OF ESCAPE

Definitions for this Chapter

A "final exit" is the termination of an escape route from a building or structure giving direct access to a place of safety such as a street, passageway, walkway or open space and sited to ensure that people can disperse safely from the vicinity of the building or structure and the effects of fire.

A "means of escape" is the structural means whereby a safe route is provided for people to travel from any point in a building or structure to a place of safety without outside assistance.

A "place of safety" is a place in which a person is no longer in danger from fire.

Introduction

12.1 This chapter is intended to assist the organiser in understanding what is necessary to ensure suitable and sufficient means of escape in case of fire for all people present. Further detailed guidance is given in the "Guide to Fire Precautions in Existing Places of Entertainment and Like Premises" (ISBN 0-11-340907-9), obtainable from HMSO, and advice may also be obtained from the fire authority for the area.

12.2 Whether the venue chosen is in a building or outdoors it is likely that some adaptation may be needed to accommodate a pop concert. This chapter is, in the main, about the means of escape which may need to be provided within buildings, sports stadia and at outdoor venues in order to safely accommodate a pop concert. It also explains about occupant capacity.

General principles for means of escape

12.3 The principle on which means of escape provisions are based is that people, regardless of the location of the fire, should be able to proceed safely along a recognisable escape route, without outside assistance, to a place of safety.

12.4 When faced with the need to evacuate a venue, people will frequently look first to the way they entered. If this cannot be reached (perhaps because of the position of the fire or smoke) they will need to be able to turn away from the fire and seek an alternative route to a place of safety. The public may nevertheless underestimate the risk or may be reluctant to use exits with which they are unfamiliar. It is essential that the training of stewards recognises this fact and that they ensure that the public leave promptly (see Chapter 3).

12.5 People should be able to walk to safety along a clearly recognisable route by their own unaided efforts regardless of where a fire may break out at the venue. It is however recognised that it will be difficult (if not impossible) for some people with disabilities to make their way to a place of safety without the assistance of others. Arrangements for people who are disabled should therefore be carefully considered and these are set out in Chapter 4.

Indoors: Buildings designed for public assembly

12.6 Buildings which have been designed for public assembly will have suitable and sufficient means of escape for their designed purpose. However adaptations such as the provision of a stage, temporary stands, or a significant increase in the number of people to be accommodated need to be taken into consideration and may require additional measures.

12.7 Where additions to the existing means of escape are necessary, the organiser should ensure that:–

- exits are suitable and sufficient in size and number;

- exits are distributed so as to allow people to turn their back on any fire which may occur;

- exits and exit routes are clearly indicated; and

- escape routes are adequately lit (see Chapter 9).

Indoors: Buildings not designed for public assembly

12.8 Because it is unlikely that such venues were designed to accommodate large numbers of people, it is almost certain that additional means of escape will be required to accommodate a pop concert. The basic principles described in paragraphs 12.3 to 12.5 will need to be met if the venue is to prove suitable. The licensing authority should be consulted at an early stage and in deciding whether the means of escape are reasonable they will take into consideration:–

- the occupant capacity of the building;

- the width and number of exits required;

- whether temporary stands and/or stages will be constructed within the building;

- exit and directional signs; and

- the normal and emergency lighting with which the building is provided.

Note: See Chapters 13 and 14 with regard to the provision of fire fighting equipment and the means for giving warning in the event of fire.

Sports stadia

12.9. A sports stadium which has been issued with a general safety certificate under the Safety of Sports Grounds Act 1975 will be provided with adequate means of escape from the normal spectator areas. However, additional exits may be needed if the pitch area is to be occupied by the public and/or by temporary structures, such as a stage or stands. If the stadium is designated under Section 1 of the 1975 Act a Special Safety Certificate is likely to be required for the event. Where such a certificate is required the event organiser should apply to the relevant local authority as early as possible.

12.10 If a sports stadium is to be used which does not require certification under the legislation described in paragraph 12.9 or Part 3 of the Fire Safety and Safety of Places of Sport Act 1987, the organiser will need to ensure that there are adequate means of escape from all areas. The licensing authority should be consulted at an early stage and further guidance in relation to the spectator and ancillary areas is given in the Guide to Safety at Sports Grounds (ISBN 0-11-341001-8).

Outdoor venues

12.11 Outdoor venues such as parks, fields and gardens of stately homes will normally have boundary fences at their perimeters. In order to provide means of escape which will allow for an orderly evacuation to take place the organiser will need to ensure that:–

- the number and size of exits in the fences etc. are sufficient for the number of   people present and are evenly distributed around the perimeter;

- exits and gateways are unlocked and staffed by stewards throughout the event; and

- all exits and gateways are clearly and conspicuously indicated and illuminated if necessary.

At the planning stage the organiser should consult the licensing authority about the proposals for means of escape.

Occupant capacity

12.12 The occupant capacity is the maximum number of people which can be safely accommodated at the venue. In the case of standing areas at longer concerts there is a need to take into account "sitting down" space for spectators and freedom of movement for access to toilets and refreshment facilities. It is essential for the organiser to agree the occupant capacity with the licensing authority as early as possible as the means of escape arrangements are dependent on this figure.

12.13 In areas where seating is provided the major part of the occupant capacity will be determined by the number of seats available. However, in other cases, a calculation will need to be made and this is based on each person occupying an area of 0.5 square metres. The maximum number of people which can be accommodated can therefore be calculated by dividing the total area available to the public (in square metres) by 0.5.

Example:– an outdoor site measuring 100 metres x 50 metres with all areas available to the public could accommodate a maximum of 10,000 people (i.e. 100 metres x 50 metres = 5000 sq metres ÷ 0.5 = 10,000).

Note: However, the enforcing authority may decide that for certain events (e.g. a "rave") the occupant capacity should be reduced.

Stairways

12.14 Any stairway, lobby, corridor or passageway, which forms part of the means of escape from the venue, should be of a uniform width and should be so constructed and arranged so as to provide a safe escape for the people using it.

12.15 In general, stairways should be about 1 metre wide and in any event should not be less than 750mm. The aggregate capacity of stairways should be sufficient for the number of people likely to have to use them at the time of a fire. In this connection it will be necessary to consider the possibility of one stairway being inaccessible because of fire and the aggregate width should allow for this possible reduction. Detailed guidance on exit capacity, related to evacuation time, is given in the document quoted in paragraph 12.1.

12.16 Stairways wider than about 2 metres should normally be divided into sections, each separated from the adjacent section by a handrail, so that each section measured between the handrails is not normally less than 1 metre wide.

Ramps

12.17 Where ramps are used:–

- the gradient should be constant and not broken by steps;

- the maximum gradient for a ramp which is subject to heavy crowd flow should not exceed 1 in 12; and

- the ramp should have a non-slip surface and, as appropriate, have a guard rail and a hand rail.

Note: Ramps installed for wheelchair users should conform to British Standard 5810.

Exits

12.18 Every venue should be provided with exits which are sufficient for the number of people present in relation to their width, number and siting. Normally no exit should be less than about 1 metre wide. Full guidance on the calculation of exit widths and evacuation times for places of public assembly is given in the "Guide to Fire Precautions in Existing Places of Entertainment and Like Premises" and for sports stadia in the "Guide to Safety at Sports Grounds".

Doors on escape routes and their fastenings

12.19 As a general principle, if a building is used for public assembly, a door used for means of escape should open in the direction of travel. The door should also:–

- not open across an escape route;

- be hung to open through not less than 90 degrees and with a swing which is clear of any change of floor level;

- be provided with a vision panel if it is hung to swing both ways; and

- if protecting an escape route, be fire-resisting, fitted with smoke seals and be self-closing.

Note: Any door which for structural reasons cannot be hung to open outwards should be locked in the fully open position at all times when the building or venue is occupied. The key should be removed to a safe place and the door should be clearly indicated with the words "TO BE SECURED OPEN WHEN THE PREMISES ARE OCCUPIED". The notice should be provided on each side of the door in a position where it can be clearly seen whether the door is in the open or closed position.

Fastenings on doors

12.20   Doors which are final exits and all doors leading to such exits should be checked by the manager before the event starts to ensure that they are unlocked, or in circumstances where security devices are provided, can be easily and immediately opened from within, without the use of a key, by persons escaping. Security fastenings such as padlocks and chains should not, under any circumstances, be used when the venue is occupied. Where such devices are used to secure the building when it is unoccupied, they should be placed on numbered hooks in a position which is not accessible to unauthorised persons at all times when the building is occupied. All fastenings should be numbered to match the numbered hooks.

12.21   Where doors have to be kept fastened while people are present, they should be fastened only by pressure release devices such as panic bolts, panic latches or pressure pads which ensure that the door can be readily opened by pressure applied by people from within. Panic bolts and panic latches should comply with British Standard 5725: Part 1.

Self-closing devices for doors

12.22   It may be necessary for escape routes to be protected by fire-resisting construction and fire doors. All such doors, except those to cupboards and service ducts, should be fitted with effective self-closing devices to ensure the positive closure of the door. Rising butt hinges are not normally acceptable. Fire doors to cupboards, service ducts and any vertical shafts linking floors should be either self-closing or should be kept locked shut when not in use and labelled accordingly.

12.23   All fire doors should be regularly checked to ensure that they are undamaged, swing freely, are closely fitted to frame and floor and that the self-closing device operates effectively.

Exit and directional signs

12.24   Because people usually leave a building by the same way that they enter or by routes which are familiar to them it is essential that all available exits are clearly indicated so that members of the audience are aware that there are ways to leave the building in an emergency other than by the doors which they used to gain admission. In addition, the provision of well sign-posted exit routes in full view of everyone present will give a feeling of security in an emergency situation.

12.25   All new fire safety signs, notices and graphic symbols should conform with British Standard 5499: Parts 1 and 3. However, existing signs and notices need not be replaced if they are fulfilling their purpose effectively.

12.26   Exit signs can take the form of a pictogram symbol or a sign bearing the words "Fire Exit" in conspicuous lettering. A fire exit symbol or sign should, wherever possible, be displayed immediately above the exit opening. Where this is not possible, a position should be chosen where the symbol or sign can be seen and is not likely to be obstructed.

12.27 Where an exit cannot be seen or where a person escaping might be in doubt as to the location of an exit, directional exit signs should be provided at suitable points along the escape route. Such signs should be sufficiently large, should be fixed in conspicuous positions, and wherever possible be positioned between 2 metres and 2.5 metres above the ground level.

12.28 Exit and directional signs should be illuminated whenever the public are present. Signs at outdoor events should be weatherproof and should be clearly visible above the audience.

Normal and emergency lighting

12.29 All parts of the venue to which the public have access and all escape routes should be provided with normal and (if used outside the hours of daylight) emergency lighting (see Chapter 9).

NOTES/AMENDMENTS

FIRE FIGHTING EQUIPMENT

Introduction

13.1 This chapter gives advice on fire fighting equipment for use in the early stages of a fire before the arrival of the fire brigade. Some venues designed for public assembly may have a fire suppression system e.g. a sprinkler system, but generally portable or hand fire fighting equipment, i.e. extinguishers, hose reels and fire blankets is all that is required by any conditions of licence.

13.2 All venues should be provided with appropriate portable or hand fire fighting equipment and this provision should be agreed at the planning stage with the licensing authority who will have liaised with the fire authority.

Classification of fires

13.3 Fires are classified in accordance with British Standard EN 2 and are defined as follows:–

Class A fires – Fires involving solid materials, usually of an organic nature, in which combustion normally takes place with the formation of glowing embers.

Class B fire – Fires involving liquids or liquefiable solids.

Class C fires – Fire involving gases.

Class D fires – Fires involving metals.

Portable equipment

13.4 If portable fire extinguishers are installed, they should conform to British Standard 5423 and be provided and allocated to comply with clause 5.2 of British Standard 5306: Part 3.

Class A fires

13.5 Class A fires are the most likely type of fire to occur in the majority of venues. Water, foam and multi purpose powder are the effective media for extinguishing these fires. Water and foam are usually considered to be the most suitable media and the appropriate equipment is therefore hose reels, water type extinguishers or extinguishers containing fluoroprotein foam (FP), aqueous film forming foam (AFFF), or film forming fluoroprotein foam (FFFP).

Hose reels

13.6 If hose reels are installed they should be located where they are conspicuous and always accessible, e.g. in corridors. The hose should comply with Type 1 hose specified in British Standard 3169 and hose reel installations should conform with British Standard 5306: Part 1 and British Standard 5274.

Class B fires

13.7   Where there is a risk of fire involving flammable liquid it will usually be appropriate to provide portable fire extinguishers of foam (including FP, AFFF and FFFP), carbon dioxide (CO_2), halon or powder types. Table 1 of clause 5.3 of British Standard 5306: Part 3 gives guidance on the minimum scale of provision of various extinguishing media for dealing with a fire involving exposed surfaces of contained liquid.

Note: Care should be taken when using halon or CO_2 extinguishers as the fumes and products of combustion may be hazardous in confined spaces. For environmental reasons it is recommended that the provision of halon extinguishers should be avoided where other suitable extinguishing media are available. However, until suitable arrangements can be made for the disposal or banking of halons, existing fire extinguishers should remain in situ.

Class C fires

13.8   No special extinguishers are made for dealing with fires involving gases because the only effective action against such fires is to stop the flow of gas by closing the valve or plugging the leak. There would be a risk of an explosion if a fire involving escaping gas were to be extinguished before the supply could be cut off.

Class D fires

13.9   None of the extinguishing media referred to in the preceding paragraphs will deal effectively with a fire involving metals such as aluminium, magnesium, sodium or potassium, although there is a special powder which is capable of controlling some Class D fires. Such fires should, however, only be tackled by specially trained personnel.

Fire blankets

13.10   Fire blankets are suitable for some types of fire. They are classified in British Standard 6575 and are described as follows:–

- *Light duty*. These are suitable for dealing with small fires in containers of cooking fat or oils and fires in clothing.

- *Heavy duty*. These are for industrial use where there is a need for the blanket to resist penetration by molten materials.

Fires involving electrical equipment

13.11 Extinguishers provided specifically for the protection of electrical risks should be of the dry powder, CO_2 or halon type. While some extinguishers containing aqueous solutions such as AFFF may meet the requirements of the electrical conductivity test of British Standard 5423 they may not sufficiently reduce the danger of conductivity along wetted surfaces such as the floor. Consequently, such extinguishers should not be provided specifically for the protection of electrical risks. See Note to paragraph 13.7.

Indoors: Buildings designed for public assembly

13.12 Normally, the scale of provision required in connection with the normal use of the building will be adequate. However, if additional facilities are to be provided e.g. a stage, concessions on a pitch, changing rooms etc. there may be a need for additional equipment.

Indoors: Buildings not designed for public assembly

13.13 These venues cause the greatest concern as existing provisions may be minimal. However, there may be some provision (e.g. hose reels in a warehouse) and provided that the maintenance is satisfactory, this should be taken into account. In deciding what fire-fighting equipment is appropriate, regard needs to be given to both the structure and the contents of the building and in considering the scale of provision, the general principle is that no-one should have to travel more than 30 metres from the site of a fire in order to reach an extinguisher. Extinguishers should be sited on exit routes near to exits.

Outdoor venues

13.14 The provision of fire fighting equipment for outdoor venues will vary according to the local conditions and what is brought on to the site. For example, there will need to be equipment for tackling fires in vegetation, vehicles and marquees. The best arrangement is to provide well indicated fire points as follows:-

- where water standpipes are provided on site and there is a water supply of sufficient pressure and flow to project a jet of water approximately 5 metres from the nozzle, fire points consisting of a standpipe together with a reel of small diameter hose of not less than 30 metres in length should be provided. The hose should be provided with the means of connection to the water standpipe (preferably a screw thread) and should terminate in a small hand control nozzle. Hoses should be housed in a box painted red and marked "HOSE REEL"; and

- where standpipes are not provided or the water pressure or flow is not sufficient, each fire point should be provided with either :–

- a water tank at least 500 litres in capacity fitted with a hinged cover , 2 buckets and 1 hand pump or bucket pump; or

- a suitable number of water type fire extinguishers (not less than 2 x 9 litres).

Note: Arrangements may need to be made to protect fire fighting equipment located outdoors from the effects of frost.

13.15 Fire points should be prominently indicated by means of conspicuous signs.

Special risks

13.16 In addition to the general provision described in paragraphs 13.13 and 13.14, portable fire fighting equipment should be provided for special risks in accordance with the following scale:–

- **Stage exceeding 56m^2**

  hydraulic hose reels or 2 water type extinguishers (rating 13A), on each side of the stage, and 1 light duty fire blanket (see below regarding electrical equipment);

- **Stage not exceeding 56m^2**

  1 water type extinguisher (rating 13A), on each side of the stage, and 1 light duty fire blanket (see below regarding electrical equipment);

- **Dressing rooms**

  in every block of 4 dressing rooms a minimum of 1 water type extinguisher (rating 13A) and 1 light duty fire blanket;

- **Scenery store, stage basement, property store and bandroom**

  1 water type extinguisher (rating 13A) in each risk area, or an appropriate extinguisher where water is unsuitable for the fire risk presented;

- **Electrical intake rooms, battery rooms, stage switchboards and electrical equipment**

  1 carbon dioxide extinguisher, or 1 dry powder extinguisher, or 1 halon extinguisher (minimum rating 21B);

- **Boiler rooms**

  - solid fuel fired – 1 water type extinguisher (rating 13A);

  - oil fired – 1 dry powder or foam extinguisher (rating 34B);

- **Portable generators (power supply)**

  1 carbon dioxide extinguisher, or 1 dry powder extinguisher, or 1 halon extinguisher (minimum rating 21B); and

- **Mobile Concessions**

  1 dry powder extinguisher (rating 21B) and 1 light duty fire blanket.

13.17 The classification of fires is described in paragraph 13.3 and in accordance with British Standard EN 2. The illustrations of portable extinguishers indicate the whole body in a colour which is the colour code for that particular type of extinguisher.

FIRE
EXTINGUISHERS

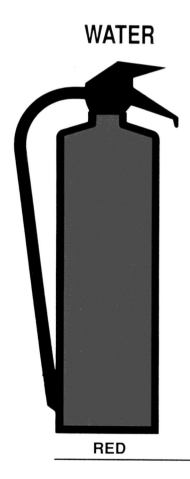

WATER

RED

EXTINGUISHING ACTION

By cooling the burning material.

CLASS OF FIRE

Class A

DANGER Do not use on live electrical equipment, burning fats or oils.

METHOD OF USE

The jet or spray should be directed at the base of the flames and kept moving across the area of the fire. Any hot spots should be sought out after the main fire is out.

FOAM
(Protein P) Type

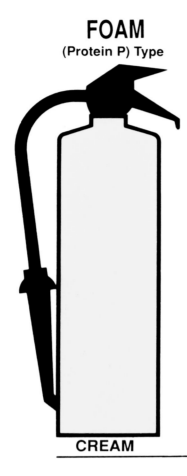

CREAM

Fluoroprotein foam (FP)

EXTINGUISHING ACTION

Forms a blanket of foam over the surface of the burning liquid and smothers the fire.

CLASS OF FIRE

Class B

DANGER Do not use on live electrical equipment.

METHOD OF USE

The jet should not be aimed directly onto the liquid. Where the liquid on fire is in a container the jet should be directed at the edge of the container or on a nearby surface above the burning liquid. The foam should be allowed to build up so that it flows across the liquid.

CREAM

Aqueous film-forming foam (AFFF)   Film-forming Fluoro-protein foam (FFFP)

EXTINGUISHING ACTION

Forms a fire extinguishing water film on the surface of the burning liquid. Has a cooling action with a wider extinguishing application than water on solid combustible materials.

CLASS OF FIRE

Classes A & B

DANGER Some extinguishers of this type are not suitable for use on live electrical equipment.

METHOD OF USE

For Class A fires the directions for water extinguishers should be followed.

For Class B fires the directions for foam extinguishers should be followed.

POWDER

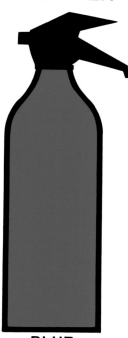

BLUE

EXTINGUISHING ACTION

Chemical inhibition of combustion.

CLASS OF FIRE

Class B

Safe on live electrical equipment although does not readily penetrate spaces inside equipment. A fire may re-ignite.

METHOD OF USE

The discharge nozzle should be directed at the base of the flames and with a rapid sweeping motion the flame should be driven towards the far edge until the flames are out. If the extinguisher has a shut-off control the air should then be allowed to clear; if the flames re-appear the procedure should be repeated.

WARNING Powder has a limited cooling effect and care should be taken to ensure the fire does not re-ignite.

POWDER (Multi-purpose)

BLUE

EXTINGUISHING ACTION

Altering the thermal decomposition to produce non-flammable products by cooling (Class A) and chemical inhibition of combustion (Class B).

CLASS OF FIRE

Classes A & B

Safe on live electrical equipment although does not readily penetrate spaces inside equipment. A fire may re-ignite.

METHOD OF USE

The discharge nozzle should be directed at the base of the flames and with a rapid sweeping motion the flame should be driven towards the far edge until the flames are out. If the extinguisher has a shut-off control the air should then be allowed to clear; if the flames re-appear the procedure should be repeated.

WARNING Powder has a limited cooling effect and care should be taken to ensure the fire does not re-ignite.

CARBON DIOXIDE (CO$_2$)

BLACK

EXTINGUISHING ACTION

Displacing oxygen in the air.

CLASS OF FIRE

Class B

Safe and clean to use on live electrical equipment.

METHOD OF USE

The discharge horn should be directed at the base of the flames and the jet kept moving across the area of the fire.

WARNING CO^2 has a limited cooling effect and care should be taken to ensure that the fire does not re-ignite.

DANGER Fumes from CO^2 extinguishers can be harmful to users in confined spaces. The area should therefore be ventilated as soon as the fire has been extinguished.

HALON

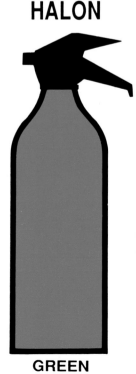

GREEN

EXTINGUISHING ACTION

Vaporising liquid gas giving rapid knock down by chemically inhibiting combustion.

CLASS OF FIRE

Class B

Clean and light. Can also be used on small surface burning Class A fires. Effective and safe on live electrical equipment.

NOTE   For environmental reasons it is recommended that the provision of halon extinguishers should be avoided where other suitable extinguishing media is available.

METHOD OF USE

The gas is expelled in a jet which should not be aimed into burning liquids as this risks spreading the fire. The discharge nozzle should therefore be aimed at the flames and kept moving across the area of the fire.

WARNING Halon has a limited cooling effect and care should be taken to ensure that the fire does not re-ignite.

DANGER Fumes from halon extinguishers can be harmful to users in confined spaces or if used on hot metal. The area should therefore be ventilated as soon as the fire has been extinguished.

HOSE REEL

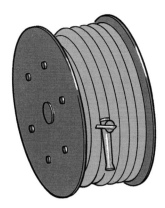

RED

EXTINGUISHING ACTION

Water - by cooling the burning material.

CLASS OF FIRE

Class A

DANGER Do not use on live electrical equipment.

METHOD OF USE

The jet should be aimed at the base of the flames and kept moving across the area of the fire. If an isolating valve is fitted it should be opened before the hose is unreeled.

RED

Light duty

Heavy duty

EXTINGUISHING ACTION

Smothering

CLASS OF FIRE

Classes A & B

Suitable for burning clothing and small fires involving burning liquids.

Suitable for industrial use.
Resistant to penetration by molten materials.

METHOD OF USE

The blanket should be placed carefully over the fire and the hands shielded from the fire. Care should be taken that the flames are not wafted towards the user or bystanders.

British Standard 5423 recommends that extinguishers should be
(a) predominantly red with a colour coded area; (b) predominantly colour coded; or (c) of self-coloured metal with a colour coded area.

MEANS FOR GIVING WARNING IN CASE OF FIRE

Introduction

14.1   This chapter is intended to give general advice to organisers on the means for giving warning in the event of fire. More detailed advice may be obtained from the guide referred to at paragraph 12.1 or from the fire authority.

Fire warning systems

14.2   The purpose of a fire warning system is to provide information to stewards and everyone present so that all can be safely evacuated before escape routes become impassable through fire, heat or smoke. The means for giving warning should be suitable for the particular venue, taking into account its size and layout and the number of people likely to be present.

14.3   Experience has shown that a conventional fire warning system of bells alone does not secure the necessary positive reaction in situations where large numbers of people are assembled. A lack of information can lead to the crowd being confused about the action they should take. To avoid such confusion and to ensure that the public respond effectively they should be given clear information. Messages may either be pre-recorded and actuated automatically on the operation of the system or given by means of a public address announcement. In either case there should be effective arrangements for silencing amplified music, preferably automatically, on the actuation of the fire alarm. (see Chapter 5).

14.4   Fire warning systems should generally comply with British Standard 5839: Part 1. Existing systems designed or installed to an earlier standard may be acceptable subject to satisfactory testing, electrical certification and approval by the licensing authority.

Indoors: Buildings designed for public assembly

14.5   A venue already licensed for pop concerts will have an approved means for giving warning in case of fire. Other venues licensed for public entertainment etc. will have a warning system which may be suitable for a pop concert. However, it will be necessary for the licensing authority to be consulted at an early stage to ensure that the system is appropriate.

Indoors: Buildings not designed for public assembly

14.6   Buildings not designed for public assembly such as disused warehouses, aircraft hangars, agricultural buildings etc may have a warning system which is unsuitable for a pop concert or no fire warning system at all. It will therefore be necessary to either modify the existing system in order to use the building for the concert or provide a temporary warning system.

14.7 If a temporary warning system is installed (and this may be the more appropriate action to take), the provision of a radio transmission system has a number of advantages as it will not require the laying of electrical wiring or modifications to a building. Static call points can also be replaced by mobile call points carried by stewards so that the alarm can be raised instantly at the point of discovery of any fire. It is, however, still necessary for any system to comply with the general principles of British Standard 5839: Part 1 and reference should also be made to British Standard 7443. The licensing authority should be consulted as to the suitability of the system for the venue.

14.8 For some buildings not designed for public entertainment, an alarm system incorporating automatic fire detection may be required, particularly in circumstances where a fire could reach serious proportions before discovery.

Outdoor events

14.9 Although there is less likelihood of people becoming trapped by fire when the event is staged outdoors it will still be necessary to provide a fire warning system for temporary and movable structures such as marquees.

NOTES/AMENDMENTS

Chapter 15

FIRE SAFETY ADVICE ON CURTAINS, DRAPES AND OTHER MATERIALS

Introduction

15.1 Organisers should be aware that the use of curtains, drapes, and temporary decorations can affect the safe use of the means of escape. Any proposal to use combustible decorative materials should be notified to the licensing authority in writing and should be accompanied by full details, including samples (not less than 1 metre by 0.5 metre) of the material proposed to be used. Where a building is already being used for public assembly the use of these materials will probably have been approved.

Curtains and drapes

15.2 All curtains and drapes should be of durable or inherently flame retarded fabric and should conform with British Standard 5867: Part 2 Fabric Type B when tested in accordance with British Standard 5438.

Note: Where doubt exists about the flame retardancy of a material the event organiser should obtain a test certificate to show compliance with the appropriate standard. Tests should be conducted by an approved laboratory under the Department of Trade and Industry's NAMAS scheme.

15.3 Curtains across exit doors present an additional problem and should be arranged so as not to trail on the floor. They should open from the centre and should only be permitted where stewards are present nearby to open the curtain in the event of an emergency.

Artificial and dried foliage

15.4 All artificial and dried foliage used for decorative purposes in public areas should be flame retardant. As the flame retardant treatment can be adversely affected by contact with moisture, periodic re-treatment may be necessary to maintain its effectiveness. Re-treatment may also be necessary to maintain the appearance of the foliage.

15.5 There are no laboratory test methods for assessing the flame retardant properties of dried or artificial foliage. However, it is recommended that these and similar items should be subject to ignition tests using small flaming sources comparable to those used for testing drapes and curtaining.

15.6 As it is difficult to totally inhibit the production of flaming molten droplets or debris from the solid plastic parts of artificial foliage such as branches and stems, the licensing authority may limit the amount of material used and prohibit use in some locations.

15.7 Dried flowers and grasses should not be sprayed with hair lacquer or similar substances, as such treatment will make them ignite more easily and burn more quickly.

NOTES/AMENDMENTS

Chapter 16

EMERGENCY PROCEDURES AND MAJOR INCIDENTS

Introduction

16.1 The consequences of an emergency at a pop concert could be catastrophic and it is necessary to plan for such an occurrence. An emergency situation will normally require a multi-disciplinary approach in which the manager, the police, the NHS including the ambulance service, the fire authority, the local Emergency Planning Officer, stewards and first aiders may all play a part. It is therefore important that there is a clear demarcation of duties and that responsibilities are agreed and understood at the planning stage. Agreed emergency procedures should be issued in writing to all relevant parties.

Incident control centre

16.2 A designated incident control centre should be provided at all large events for use by senior personnel from the management team, police and fire authorities, the ambulance service, first aid organisations, the local authority and stewards. A dedicated external telephone line should be provided. The centre should be able to make an announcement which is directly conveyed by the public address system.

16.3 Back-up power and lighting services should be provided to the incident control centre.

16.4 The centre should have a copy of the gridded site plan indicating all services.

16.5 Although the police will generally offer advice, the manager is normally responsible for dealing with most emergencies which could occur and for making appropriate decisions. The organiser will need to establish at the planning stage the circumstances in which the police would take over control for the handling of an emergency.

Emergency evacuation plan

16.6 An emergency evacuation plan should be drawn up by the event organiser in liaison with the emergency services and the licensing authority. The plan should provide arrangements for:–

- identification of key decision-making personnel;

- stopping the concert;

- identification of emergency routes;

- identification of holding areas for performers, employees and the audience;

- details of the script of coded messages to alert and "stand down" management and stewards;

- details of the script of public address announcements to the audience;

- identification of rendezvous points for emergency services;

- identification of ambulance loading points and triage areas;

- details of hospitals in the area prepared for major incidents and secure traffic routes to such hospitals;

- details of a temporary mortuary facility; and

- an outline of the roles of those involved.

16.7 People making emergency announcements should work from a prepared script and be practised in doing so. Performers should not have primary responsibility for making announcements but their assistance may be useful in providing information to the audience.

Major incidents

16.8 A major incident is any emergency which requires the implementation of special arrangements by one or more of the emergency services, the NHS or the local authority in order to:-

- rescue, treat and transport a large number of casualties; and

- handle a large number of enquiries from the public and/or the news media.

In planning for such an emergency, it is suggested that reference should be made to the Home Office publication "Dealing with Disaster", ISBN 0-11-341044-1.

16.9 All emergency services have a procedures manual for major incidents. However, a specific operational plan will be necessary for a large pop concert. This plan should be drawn up at the event planning meeting following consultation between the emergency services, the organiser and other interested parties. The aim of the plan will be to allow the emergency services and the manager of the event to react quickly and efficiently to a major incident. The plan should be seen as a guide to the action required and should allow for flexibility in the response.

16.10 The police will normally be responsible for the co-ordination of the overall response to a major incident. This co-ordination will assist in the effective operation of all the emergency services. The fire brigade will be responsible for matters concerning fire and rescue and the ambulance service will be responsible for providing emergency treatment at the scene, triage and transporting the injured to hospital.

16.11 If there are fatalities, the police may have a responsibility to investigate the cause of death and treat the scene as a scene of crime. Investigation of the cause is a statutory duty in Scotland. In these circumstances, the scene must, as far as possible, be carefully preserved. A temporary mortuary facility should be designated prior to the event and it is important that the building chosen fulfils its purpose and to achieve this, the coroner for the area should be consulted. It may also be helpful to designate rendezvous points, a waiting area for relatives and a media liaison point. The names of any fatalities and any people who are injured and/or taken to hospital should be carefully recorded.

16.12 Emergency access routes to and within the site should be readily identifiable which, in the event of a major incident, will be controlled by police officers to ensure clear routes for emergency vehicles.

NOTES/AMENDMENTS

PART IV

VENUE FACILITIES

Chapter 17

TRAFFIC AND TRANSPORT ARRANGEMENTS

Introduction

17.1 A pop concert can have a significant effect on road traffic and public transport before, during, and after the event. If the transport arrangements are not carefully planned, the consequences can range from delays for the audience and inconvenience for local residents to substantial disruption of the local transport system and the prevention of access for the emergency services to the concert site and other areas. It is therefore essential that arrangements for the movement of traffic are discussed and agreed with the police and other interested organisations at the planning stage.

17.2 A full assessment is needed of the likely impact of the concert so that suitable arrangements can be made to manage the arrival and dispersal of the audience and ensure that car and coach parking facilities are adequate. The police and motoring organisations should be consulted about the signposting of the routes and the proposed arrangements for routing and access for the emergency services. Contact with the railway authorities may also be necessary.

17.3 The event organiser should, if appropriate, seek advice from bus/coach organisations regarding the opportunities for using shuttle arrangements between the site and remote car parks or railway stations, etc.

Traffic marshalling and signposting

17.4 The following factors should be taken into consideration:–

- there should be satisfactory arrangements for marshalling traffic and the control of access and egress from official car parks should be arranged in consultation with the police;

- there should be sufficient marshals (stewards) who should manage the traffic flows to and from the event and have responsibility for directing the parking of vehicles within designated areas;

- the need for satisfactory communication between marshals and the police;

- the need for the parking arrangements and access and egress routes to be adequately signposted. This should be arranged in consultation with the motoring organisations and the police; and

- the need to ensure that routes to the venue are adequately signposted and remain so until the event is over.

Emergency access

17.5 There should be adequate provision for emergency vehicles to access the site at all times. Internal routes should be kept clear, including such routes within car parks. Access to hydrants and other water supplies should not be obstructed.

17.6 The site chosen should allow adequate means of access by the fire brigade to within 45 metres to 50 metres of any structure including fuel storage facilities. The access route will need to bear the weight of fire appliances and in particular a route containing manhole covers should be avoided. Table 1 sets out the generally accepted parameters relating to access for fire appliances. The organiser should ensure at the planning stage that access roads are suitable. Where access routes to and within the site are accessible via bridges, the weight restriction of the bridge should be not less than the weight of the appliance expected to use it. Turning facilities should also be provided in any dead-end access route which is longer than 20m.

Table 1 Fire appliance access route specification

Appliance Type	Minimum Width of Road metres	Minimum Width of Gateway metres	Minimum Turning Circle metres	Minimum Clearance Height (m) metres	Minimum Carrying Capacity metres
Pump	3.7	3.1	16.8	3.7	12.5
High Reach	3.7	3.1	29.0	4.0	17.0

17.7 Wherever practicable, roads within 300 metres of the venue should be kept entirely free of parking so as not to delay or obstruct emergency vehicles.

Pedestrian access

17.8 Adequate and sufficient access routes for pedestrians should be provided to and from the site and these should be well lit. The access routes should not cross car or coach parks and should also avoid the need to cross traffic routes.

Public transport

17.9 The availability of adequate public transport and the estimated arrival and departure times of the audience should be discussed with the police and the appropriate transport authorities well in advance of the date of the concert.

17.10 For large outdoor and major indoor events, the use of existing or specially provided public transport systems should be encouraged, particularly where it is likely that the audience will consist of young people. It may be useful if arrangements can be made with coach and bus operators for the temporary diversion of vehicles from normal routes in order to connect with a shuttle bus service. Information should be available inside the site informing people of the times of shuttle buses, especially the last service. Details of the transport arrangements should be advertised and these may include:–

Railways
the provision of additional trains, as maximising their use will limit the demand for on-site car parking. This option should take into account the distance of the station from the venue and the availability of connecting bus and coach services.
    The advice of rail authorities should be sought in relation to the maximum number of people that a station can accommodate.

Coaches

a "package" deal with coach companies which includes the cost of travel and admission ticket.

Buses

a "park and ride" bus system from remote car parks and the provision of single deck buses, as these are generally easier to exit from. Boarding points should be clearly indicated and adequately lit. If scheduled bus services operate, it would be useful if the organiser can arrange with the company for a more frequent service at the beginning and end of the event.

Parking

17.11   Procedures for parking cars, coaches and other vehicles should be arranged to reduce the possibility of road congestion and disruption. The location of car and coach parks should be indicated on tickets or in advertising for the concert.

17.12   Car and coach parks should be adequately lit, signposted and labelled, with reflective numerals or letters, so that vehicles can be easily located. Where practicable, car and coach parks should be segregated.

17.13   For outdoor events, reminder signs should be positioned at exit gates leading from the parking areas to the venue, to assist in identifying where cars have been parked.

17.14   Wherever practicable, parking on soft ground should be avoided. Where this is not possible, or the ground may become soft from rain, a suitable number of towing vehicles should be provided. If possible, the organiser should arrange with the motoring organisations for facilities to be provided to assist people who are unable to start their vehicles.

Outdoor events

17.15   Among the factors to be considered for such events and discussed at the planning stage are:–

- a system of entrance gate numbers, car park identification numbers or colours;
- emergency vehicle rendezvous points;
- motoring organisation points;
- use of temporary traffic lights;
- telephones;
- pick up and set down points for taxis and private cars;
- shuttle bus boarding/disembarkation points; and
- sanitary accommodation in car parks.

17.16   The organiser may also need to consider if a helipad should be provided to assist in an emergency and for the use of special guests.

17.17   Details of traffic arrangements should be publicised in advance and the media should be alerted.

NOTES/AMENDMENTS

MEDICAL/FIRST AID PROVISION

Definitions for this Chapter

A "qualified medical practitioner" is a medical practitioner registered with the General Medical Council who has knowledge and experience of accident and emergency work.

A "qualified nurse" is a nurse whose name is entered in Part 1, 2, 7 or 12 of the professional register maintained by the United Kingdom Central Council for Nursing, Midwifery and Health Visiting and who has post-registration knowledge and experience of accident and emergency work.

A "paramedic" is a person who holds a current certificate of proficiency in ambulance paramedical skills issued by or with the approval of the Secretary of State for Health/Secretary of State for Scotland.

A "first aider" is a fully trained person who holds a current certificate of first aid competency issued by any of the three voluntary bodies, i.e. St John Ambulance, British Red Cross Society or St Andrew's Ambulance Association.

Introduction

18.1 The number of people requiring first aid treatment at a pop concert will vary considerably as will the type of ailment. These can range from cuts and bruises to dehydration, sunstroke, hyperventilation, crushing injuries and unconsciousness. People with asthma, heart problems, diabetes, etc. attend concerts and their condition may be exacerbated or, in extreme cases, their lives may be put at risk. It is therefore essential that all concerts have adequate first aid arrangements and the organiser will need to ensure that the first aid provision is approved by the licensing authority.

Planning

18.2 The organiser of large events should, at the planning stage, consult the local NHS Chief Ambulance Officer on the ambulance and first aid requirements. The organiser should also consult whichever organisations are providing first aid cover, e.g. St John Ambulance Brigade, British Red Cross Society, St Andrew's Ambulance Association and the details of the event should be confirmed in writing to the first aid organisation as soon as possible but no later than four weeks before the event.

Note : In Scotland the organiser should also consult the local Health Board regarding the overall provision of both medical and first aid facilities.

18.3 A senior officer of the organisation providing first aid should be appointed to take overall control and co-ordination of first aid provision. He or she should liaise with the senior officer of the Ambulance Service if they attend the event and any medical practitioners who are present. The name and contact telephone number of this person should be made available to the local NHS Chief Ambulance Officer.

Note : In the event of a major incident, members of the voluntary agencies will be under the control of the NHS Ambulance Incident Officer.

First aid provision

18.4 The number of first aid staff which will be required will be dependent upon a number of factors, including:–

- the nature of the venue and its facilities and procedures;

- the length of the concert;

- the number expected to attend;

- the anticipated nature of the audience, including age range and male and female ratio, etc;

- previous experience of the performers' concerts; and

- whether the audience is standing or seated.

18.5 The recommended minimum numbers of first aiders for concerts where it is not considered that there is a likelihood of major audience problems are :–

- 1:500 for the first 3,000 attending and then 1:1,000 for the remainder attending.

Note: No event should have less than two first-aiders.

18.6 The following table gives examples of the number suggested for a selection of audience sizes. It also includes guidelines for the minimum number of first aid posts and ambulances which will be needed. At indoor venues which are licensed for public entertainment, first aid facilities are likely to have been agreed by the licensing authority and these may differ from the figures in the table.

Table 2 First Aid provision

Audience size	First Aiders	First Aid Posts	Ambulances
500	2	1	–
3,000	6	1	1
5,000	8	1	1
10,000	13	2	2
20,000	23	3	2–3
40,000	43	4	3–4
60,000	63	4	3–4

18.7 For higher risk events such as those attended by a very young audience or long concerts, the number of first aiders may need to be significantly increased. In these circumstances, the ambulance provision required should be discussed with the local NHS Chief Ambulance Officer, who may decide that there should be an ambulance control unit, particularly at larger events. There should be close liaison between the organiser/manager and the Chief Ambulance Officer before and during the event.

18.8 At some events, many of the members of the audience who require treatment will be in the under 16 age group and, while first aid as such may not always be required, there may be a need to treat various forms of hysteria or hyperexcitability.

18.9 At certain concerts, including higher risk events, there should be in addition to the first aiders at least 1 qualified medical practitioner. This person should be trained in cardiac pulmonary resuscitation and the injuries which could occur at a pop concert and should be familiar with the effects of alcohol and other drugs. The medical practitioner should also know the major incident plan for the area in which the event is to take place. At such events, there should be at least 2 qualified nurses for each 10,000 persons. At higher risk events, it is likely that paramedics will also be required in the pit area. It is recommended that at events attended by more than 15,000 persons, 4 paramedics should be included in the pit team.

Note: In Scotland the medical practitioner must be acceptable to the local Health Board as being competent to handle the type of problems which may arise at a large public event. The medical practitioner must also be fully familiar with the local NHS emergency plans for the handling of major incidents in the area.

First aid posts

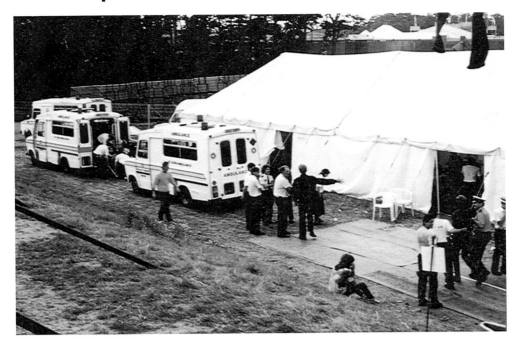

18.10 The organiser should seek advice on the number and location of first aid posts from the appropriate first aid organisation. For outdoor events, if a suitable permanent structure is not available, there should be fully equipped mobile first aid units or marquees with appropriate flooring. For indoor events, the first aid post(s) should be provided in or adjacent to the main arena, should be of adequate size and should be readily accessible for admission of casualties and ambulance crew. Advice should also be sought from the local NHS Chief Ambulance Officer.

18.11 First aid arrangements should be in position one hour before the gates or doors are open. Each first aid point should be clearly identified by a conspicuous sign and all stewards should be aware of its position. Consideration should also be given to the visibility of signs at night if this is appropriate.

18.12 Telephone and radio contact should be established between the event manager, the event safety co-ordinator, and the main first aid centre/incident control centre. At large events, consideration should be given to the need for a separate radio channel.

18.13 At large events, a first aid post should be provided near to the stage area and there should be unrestricted access to this post from the pit area. In general it is recommended that other first aid posts are situated in positions on the perimeter of the audience area, enabling unrestricted access and egress for ambulances.

18.14 There should be agreement at the planning stage on the respective roles of paramedics, first aiders and the pit team to ensure that the areas of responsibility are clear. For audiences in excess of 25,000, a designated large marquee or equivalent suitable facility (outdoor events) or large room (indoor events) should be provided for use as a casualty clearing station. This should be determined in agreement with the licensing authority.

18.15 Each first aid post should be maintained in a clean and hygienic condition, free from dust and be adequately heated, lit and ventilated. It should contain adequate blankets, pillows, stretchers, couches, buckets, bowls, trolleys and screens. A WC should be in close proximity and accessible. First aid posts should also have :–

- a supply of hot and cold water or, if this is not possible in the case of an outdoor event, sterile water or sterile normal saline; and

- a supply of drinking water over a sink or wash-hand basin.

18.16 If there is more than one first aid post, there should be a designated main first aid post with an external telephone line. All other first aid posts should have an internal telephone or radio link to the main post. All radio communication should be co-ordinated. If the local NHS ambulance service is present on the site there should be a radio communication link to their onsite control and via that to the ambulance service central control. If the ambulance service is not present, they should be consulted about the necessary communications link.

18.17 Each first aid post should be staffed by a sufficient number of competent first aiders, wearing distinctive authorised clothing, some of whom should be available to offer assistance within spectator areas. At large outdoor events, a proportion of the first aiders should be strategically positioned around the site and should be in radio contact with the fully equipped main first aid point.

18.18 The organiser of the event should ensure that the nominated first aid organisation keeps a record of all people requiring first aid treatment. This record should include the onward destination of casualties (e.g. home, hospital, own GP) and should be kept readily available for inspection by the relevant authorities. Serious cases should be reported immediately to the main first aid post and also, without delay, to the incident control centre, who may need to be aware of a pending emergency.

Clinical waste

18.19 The first aid organisation should make suitable arrangements for the disposal of clinical waste. Special containers should be provided for medical staff to dispose of "sharps" such as hypodermic needles.

First aid for employees

18.20 Under the Health and Safety (First Aid) Regulations 1981, employers are responsible for ensuring that first aid facilities are provided for their employees. First aid staff appointed to provide these facilities must have the necessary competence and training to meet the requirements of the Regulations. The organiser of the concert may find it helpful to have a written agreement between the various employers involved in the event so that there is provision for one first aid service to meet all their needs.

NOTES/AMENDMENTS

INFORMATION AND WELFARE SERVICES

Introduction

19.1   The event organiser will need to be able to provide information to the audience as this will help the concert to run smoothly and play a vital part in dealing with any emergency. The information required and the method of providing it will vary according to the concert. Public address announcements are an important method of conveying information and any messages should be clear and concise (see Chapter 9).

Information

19.2   The information required will fall broadly into two categories:–

- information on concert-related activities i.e. events, workshops, displays, entertainment, location of services, sanitary conveniences, telephone, etc; and

- information on what is available in the local area, i.e. doctors, chemists, hospitals, transport, dentists, banks, police station, social services, accommodation, shops, etc.

19.3   While large, outdoor events will require most of this information to be provided, the need at smaller, indoor concerts will be more limited. The following are examples of ways in which the information can be provided, mainly for larger events:–

- **Site plans**

  Site plans should be large, clear, waterproof, conspicuously sited at entrances, information points and first aid points and should show:–

  - sanitary conveniences;

  - stage;

  - camping area;

  - exits and entrances;

  - car parks;

  - main roads;

  - first aid points;

  - emergency services;

  - welfare points;

  - police point;

  - catering facilities;

  - lost persons' meeting point;

  - public telephones;

  - children's play area;

  - lost property; and

  - drinking water.

- **Programmes**

  When available, these should include the times and locations of events, a site plan and local information, details of what may or may not be admitted to the site, and, if appropriate, health warnings about noise levels. Details of emergency procedures could also be included.

- **Information point**

  An information point can provide people with general information and advice. This should be sited in a "quiet" area and be easily accessible.

- **Signposting**

  Services etc should be clearly and conspicuously signposted from all parts of the venue.

- **Ticket information**

  Information on tickets should be clear and precise. Retained stubs should contain as much information as possible to guide the holder once inside the venue.

19.4 The information on the admission ticket could include:–

- facilities for people with disabilities;

- restrictions on bottles, cans, etc. being brought into the venue;

- a site plan;

- a warning that prolonged exposure to loud music can damage hearing;

- any restrictions on admittance, e.g. children under the age of 5; and

- advice on where to meet for people who are lost.

Lost property

19.5 Arrangements should be made for the secure storage and retrieval of lost property, if necessary, in liaison with the police.

Meeting point

19.6 Provision should be made at all events for people who have lost their friends to be reunited.

Arrangements for children

19.7 At large outdoor events, a children's area should be provided. This should be in a quiet part of the site and be provided with appropriate amusements and supervision.

Drug counselling and befriending

19.8 At large concerts the event organiser should encourage the presence of organisations such as the Samaritans and drug counsellors. At the planning stage, it is recommended that there should be liaison with Festival Welfare Services.

Public telephones

19.9 Public telephones should be available at the venue and should be situated in a quiet area. This is particularly important if "pass outs" are not available.

"Crash" marquee

19.10 The organiser should consider the provision of a "crash" marquee which can provide emergency accommodation for members of the audience who are left without transport home or for those who arrive in advance of the event. If such a marquee is provided, it will be necessary to consider whether first aid, sanitary facilities or refreshments should be available while the marquee is in use.

NOTES/AMENDMENTS

FOOD, REFRESHMENTS AND DRINKING WATER

Food and refreshments

20.1   The organiser should ensure that all delivery, storage, preparation and sales of food comply with the appropriate legislation and that traders are reminded of the need to comply with the law. Details of all concessions should be agreed in advance with the Environmental Health Department of the relevant local authority.

20.2   At most events, a selection of food and refreshments should be made available and the needs of those people requiring special diets, e.g. diabetics, should be considered.

20.3   No food or drink should be sold or distributed in glass bottles, cans or in any other receptacle capable of causing injury to any member of the audience.

20.4   No vehicle used for dispensing food and drinks etc, should be moved whilst members of the public are present and such vehicles and any stall, kiosk, etc. should be positioned well away from the stage exit and exit routes. There should be adequate arrangements for the replenishment of stocks and the disposal of waste. Concessions will require access to a water supply.

Sale of alcohol

20.5   If it is intended to sell alcohol at the event, the organiser will require a separate licence from the licensing magistrates. The licensing authority may also stipulate conditions in relation to bar opening hours, types of container to be used, etc.

Drinking water

20.6   The provision of free drinking water is of particular importance at concerts and "raves" where the audience can be assembled in hot, cramped conditions. In such circumstances, dehydration can be a serious problem, often leading to fainting, collapse and the potential risk of being trampled.

20.7   A plentiful supply of clean drinking water from a minimum of two water points should be provided in the pit area, together with an adequate supply of paper or plastic cups (a minimum of 3,000 is suggested for large events). The water points should not be within reach of the public. If storage containers are used for the water, these should be clean and provided in sufficient numbers to allow the stewards easy access.

20.8   A sufficient number of drinking water outlets should be distributed throughout the venue. A supply of drinking water should be available at the first aid points and immediately adjacent to (but not inside) sanitary conveniences. A separate supply of water should also be available for food vending points.

20.9   At outdoor sites, one outlet should be provided for every 3,000 persons and the amount provided should take account of wastage and catering and backstage requirements. All drinking water outlets should have unobstructed access, be clearly marked and should be lit at night. To avoid the ground becoming waterlogged each tap should be self-closing and the ground adjacent to and surrounding the tap should be absorbent and well drained. If there is a camp site, water for cooking should be made available.

20.10 Water should normally be provided through a mains supply, but if this is not possible, barrels and bowsers should be used. All connections and services should be checked and maintained.

NOTES/AMENDMENTS

Chapter 21

SANITARY ACCOMMODATION

General

21.1 Organisers should ensure that adequate sanitary conveniences are provided for the number of people expected and that consideration is given to their location, access, construction and signage. They should not be situated in the vicinity of food stands.

21.2 To minimise crowding and queuing problems, sanitary conveniences should, where possible, be located at different points around the venue rather than concentrated in a small area. In deciding on the location, the need for access for servicing and emptying should be taken into account.

21.3 Ideally, sanitary conveniences should be connected to the mains drainage system. However, if this restricts the required distribution, non-mains conveniences should be used. If trenches are to be dug, consideration needs to be given to local conditions which may require the use of holding tanks.

21.4 Where temporary sanitary accommodation is required, temporary mains units should be provided if a sewer or drain and an adequate water supply is available. If this is not possible, individual non-flushable units should be considered. If self-contained portable flush units are used, suitable arrangements should be made for emptying the tanks of these units on a regular basis to prevent overflowing.

21.5 Sanitary conveniences should be constructed in such a way that people are protected from inclement weather and tripping hazards. The floor should have a non-slip surface.

21.6 An adequate supply of toilet paper should be provided in a holder or dispenser.

21.7 Sanitary conveniences should be readily visible and clearly signposted from all parts of the venue. They should be well lit at night (50 lux minimum). It may also be necessary to provide lighting during the day.

21.8 Sanitary conveniences should be regularly serviced to ensure that they are kept clean and hygienic. A sufficient number of attendants should be provided for this purpose and to prevent misuse. Arrangements should be made for the rapid clearances of any blockages to the drainage systems. Chemical closets will require regular maintenance and there should be sufficient people to undertake this work.

Number of sanitary conveniences

21.9 Minimum numbers of sanitary conveniences for cinemas, concert halls, theatres and similar buildings used for public entertainment are set out in table 7 of British Standard 6465: Part 1.

21.10 In other circumstances, the sanitary accommodation to be provided will depend on the nature of the event and the type of venue. In some situations British Standard 6465 may be appropriate. If it is not, an estimate should be made of audience size and the anticipated male/female ratio. When there is insufficient information to assess this ratio, it should be assumed that there will be a 50:50 male/female split.

Note: A company with experience at these events over a number of years has suggested that the following formula is suitable :–

- **Female conveniences**
  1 WC per 100 females.

- **Male conveniences**
  1 WC for 100 or less males;
  2 WCs for 101–500 males;
  3 WCs for 501–1000 males; +

  1 WC for every additional 500 males; and
  1.5 metres of urinal accommodation per 500 males.

The above figures are then reduced in the following way for shorter concerts :–

Duration of concert	Percentage of above standard
More than 8 hours	*100%*
6 hours but less than 8 hours	*80%*
4 hours but less than 6 hours	*75%*
Less than 4 hours	*70%*

21.11 When, at a permanent venue, the audience consists mainly of women, the organiser should consider making most of the toilets for men temporarily available to women. This accommodation should be clearly labelled.

Wash-hand basins

21.12 Where possible, wash-hand basins should be provided in the following ratio:–

- 1 per 5 sanitary conveniences (WCs and urinals).

Where slab urinals are used, each 600mm length equates to one space or urinal bowl. The nature of the site and facilities may therefore mean that a lower ratio of wash-hand basins is necessary. It is suggested that this should not be less than 1:10 sanitary conveniences. Consideration should also be given to the use of washing troughs.

21.13 Each wash-hand basin should be provided with bacteriocidal soap or antiseptic hand-wipes where hot water is not provided. Suitable drying facilities should be available. If paper towels are supplied, arrangements should be made for their regular disposal.

People with disabilities

21.14 Appropriate sanitary accommodation should be provided for wheelchair users. The water closet(s) and associated fitments including wash-hand basins should be sited close to any area set aside for wheelchair users and should be designed to comply with the provisions of British Standard 5810:1979 "Access for the Disabled to Buildings – General Recommendations". A minimum of 1 unisex water closet should be provided for venues which have a capacity of up to 2000. The provision of additional water closets should relate to the expected numbers of those attending in wheelchairs. It is suggested that 1 WC with wash-hand basin should be provided for each 100 disabled persons.

Sanitary towels

21.15 Suitable provision will be needed for disposing of used sanitary towels. A bin should be provided in each female WC compartment and arrangements should be made for these to be emptied as necessary. The provision of sanitary towels should also be considered.

Facilities for employees

21.16 Under the Workplace (Health, Safety and Welfare) Regulations 1992, suitable and sufficient sanitary conveniences and washing facilities must be provided at workplaces. HSE's Approved Code of Practice gives guidance on the facilities which should be provided.

21.17 Sanitary accommodation for use by employees etc. should be sited near to work areas and, in particular, behind the stage and near to the mixing tower, catering areas and car parks.

NOTES/AMENDMENTS

Chapter 22:   WASTE DISPOSAL

General

22.1   Waste at pop concerts can include such items as food and drink containers, plastic sheeting and paper and left-over food. Food refuse particularly can cause health and safety problems because of the risk of attracting insects etc. The accumulation of paper and boxes can cause an obstruction and may be a fire hazard. There are likely to be greater problems at outdoor events.

22.2   A sufficient number of easily identifiable, readily accessible receptacles for refuse (e.g. bins or skips) should be provided at outdoor venues. Arrangements should be made for the regular collection of refuse during the event and for its removal to an agreed and attended position. The organiser should consider the provision of receptacles outside the venue. If it is likely that receptacles will be misused and the organiser decides not to provide them, some other means should be used to ensure that refuse is regularly collected.

22.3   In particular, waste bins should be sited near to the areas where there is likely to be the greatest concentration of refuse, e.g. refreshment areas, sanitary conveniences and any camp site. The siting of waste bins should allow for easy collection (e.g. by an inner access route).

22.4   The organiser will need to consider the type of receptacle which will be provided for refuse. There are 3 main types:–

- skips which hold a large quantity of refuse in one area but have the disadvantage that litter has to be carried further and that their contents can contain a mix of items which may present a fire hazard;

- smaller receptacles which can be more easily distributed around the site, and are therefore more accessible, but have the disadvantage of being time-consuming to empty and can fall into disrepair; and

- plastic or paper sacks which are cheap to provide and can be distributed widely but are easily damaged.

22.5   The organiser should also make arrangements to clear up refuse which has been blown around the site or deposited indiscriminately.

Handling of waste

22.6   The organiser should ensure that people handling waste are provided with suitable protective equipment, particularly gloves. Special arrangements should be made for clearing around sanitary accommodation. Particular care should be taken in handling discarded hypodermic needles and syringes.

NOTES/AMENDMENTS

APPENDICES

LEGISLATION

1   Pop concerts, like other work activities, are subject to various legislation. The main Acts which regulate health, safety and welfare are the Health and Safety at Work etc. Act 1974 (HSW Act) and various Acts covering public entertainment licensing law.

2   Most health and safety legislation is qualified by the duty to take action "so far as is reasonably practicable". "Reasonably practicable" means that the time, trouble, cost and physical difficulty of taking measures to avoid the risk are not wholly disproportionate to it. The size or financial position of the employer is not taken into account in this calculation. Under licensing law, a different concept applies. The licensing authority may impose conditions which are governed by a duty of "reasonableness". This means that it can impose requirements which will achieve higher standards than those required under health and safety legislation.

The Health & Safety at Work etc. Act 1974 (HSW Act)

3   The HSW Act aims to secure the health, safety and welfare of people at work and to protect people other than those at work against risks to health and safety arising out of work activities.

4   To do this, it imposes duties on everyone concerned with work activities, ranging from employers, the self-employed and employees, to manufacturers, designers, suppliers and importers of materials for use at work, people in control of premises and members of the public.

5   The duties are expressed in general terms, so that they apply to all types of work activity and situations. In some cases, the general duties have been supplemented by specific requirements laid down in Regulations made under the Act.

6   **Section 2** of the Act is concerned with the duties of employers to their employees. The general duty is to ensure, so far as is reasonably practicable, the health, safety and welfare at work of all employees. Some of the most important areas covered by this general duty are specified. This section also requires every employer who employs 5 or more workers to prepare a written statement of safety policy setting out the organisation and arrangements in force for carrying out that policy.

7   **Section 2** also requires an employer to ensure, so far as is reasonably practicable, that workers are trained to carry out their work without risk to their health and safety.

8   **Section 3** places a duty on employers and the self-employed to safeguard those not in their employment, the public for example, who could be affected by the conduct of their undertaking.

9   **Section 4** places a duty on those who have control, to any extent, of non-domestic premises (or of plant etc. on such premises) to ensure, so far as is reasonably practicable, the premises (or plant, etc.) are safe and without risks to health of those who work there (other than their own employees).

10 **Section 6** sets out the legal duties of designers, manufacturers, importers and suppliers to produce or provide articles and substances which are, so far as reasonably practicable, safe and without risk to health when used at work.

11 **Section 7** requires employees to take reasonable care of the health and safety of themselves and others.

Application of the HSW Act to pop concerts

12 Under health and safety legislation, an event organiser, concert promoter, licensee, specialist contractor and venue owner all have a statutory duty to protect the health and safety of their workers and others who may be affected by their work activity. Employers must assess the hazards which are involved and quantify the risks which these hazards present. Wherever possible, hazards should be removed: if they cannot be removed, then they must be managed so that they do not present risks to the health and safety of workers and members of the public. This management may include, for example, the use of protective equipment such as ear protectors or the provision of a safety barrier in front of the stage.

13 **Section 2** applies to all organisations with employees at the pop concert venue including contractors, engineers, construction companies.

14 **Section 3** applies to everyone involved in the staging of a pop concert. Event organisers should ensure that they are doing all they reasonably can to protect the public. They may have no employees at the venue but their duty to safeguard third parties will extend, for example, to providing relevant information to workers about aspects of their undertaking which may affect their health and safety, such as emergency procedures. Contractors, for example, should consider what effect their work may have on the safety of the employees of other companies and on the public.

15 **Section 4** is relevant to both indoor and outdoor pop concerts. The primary responsibility for the elimination of risks will usually fall to the event organiser, the manager, the owner of the venue, licensee and/or promoter, depending upon the contractual arrangements under which the pop concert is to be run. The control of the venue may be shared between a number of parties and if this is the case, there should be liaison arrangements to ensure that responsibilities are adequately identified and assigned. Organisations and individuals who have control, to any extent, should consider what measures they can take to ensure that the venue is safe.

16 **Section 6** is particularly relevant to suppliers of equipment or substances for use at work. It also applies to designers and suppliers of equipment for use by performers etc. and to contractors who erect or install stages and sound systems.

17 **Sections 7 & 8** describe broad duties which will apply to all employees at a pop concert venue.

Risk assessment

18 The Management of Health and Safety at Work Regulations came into force on 1 January 1993. They require all employers and self-employed persons to assess the risks to workers and any others who may be affected by their undertaking.

19 A risk assessment is a systematic general examination of the work activity. It involves identifying the hazards present (whether arising from work activities or from other factors, e.g. the layout of the venue) and then evaluating the extent of the risks, taking into account whatever precautions have already been taken.

20 There are six steps which need to be taken to assess the risks associated with staging the event:–

- identify the hazards associated with activities contributing to the event, where the event is carried out and how the activities are to be undertaken;

- identify those exposed to the hazards;

- evaluate the risks, taking account of existing precautions (this will indicate the level of residual risk);

- devise a safe system of work (see below) which reduces the residual risks to as low a level as is reasonably practicable;

- implement the system of work; and

- monitor, review and revise the system as necessary to maintain its effectiveness.

A safe system of work

21 A "safe system of work" is a measure which reflects one of the general Health & Safety at Work etc. Act 1974 (HSW Act) requirements to ensure the safety of persons by eliminating or controlling residual risks to a minimum. The measures necessary in a safe system depend to a considerable extent on the work activity involved. It may include a range of precautions from simple procedures and protective equipment through to a full written permit to work. A systematic, imaginative but essentially practical risk assessment of the job and its hazards, which incorporates lessons learnt from past experience, is how employers should approach the development of a safe system.

22 It is suggested that all the operations involved in the staging of a pop concert should form part of a safe system of work. The event organiser, manager and safety co-ordinator will have a particularly important role in ensuring that this is the case.

Entertainment licensing law

23 The legislation which may be relevant in relation to licensing law includes:–

(i)   Schedule 1 to the Local Government (Miscellaneous Provisions) Act 1982;

(ii)   Schedule 12 to the London Government Act 1963;

(iii) Section 41 of the Civic Government (Scotland) Act 1982;

which have all been amended by Part IV of the Fire Safety and Safety of Places of Sport Act 1987;

(iv)   the Licensing Act 1964, as amended by the Licensing Act 1988;

(v)   the Licensing (Scotland) Act 1976;

(vi)   Private Places of Entertainment (Licensing) Act 1967; and

(vii) relevant local acts.

England & Wales

24 Under the Local Government (Miscellaneous Provisions) Act 1982 or, in Greater London, the London Government Act 1963, responsibility for controlling places which are used for **public** music and dancing and similar entertainments, including pop concerts, is vested in the district council or, in the case of London, the relevant London borough. It is normally an offence to organise public entertainment without a licence obtained in advance from the local authority, or to be in breach of any of the terms, conditions or restrictions the legislation empowers the authority to place on such a licence.

25 The purpose of this licensing regime is to ensure, amongst other things, that places of entertainment have adequate standards of safety and hygiene, and to minimise any possible nuisance which may be caused to the immediate neighbourhood. In considering public entertainment licence applications, the local authority will generally have regard to comments from the police and the fire authority, to whom advance notification of the application must be supplied.

26 The licensing of public entertainment applies to events held indoors throughout the country and also to those held outdoors in Greater London. Outside Greater London, licensing applies only to outdoor musical events on private land, and then only if the local authority has taken the necessary steps to adopt the relevant provisions of the 1982 Act.

27 Local authorities have very wide discretion over whether or not to grant entertainment licences and, in the case of indoor events or outdoor events held in Greater London, to attach to any licence such terms, conditions and restrictions as they think fit. For outdoor musical events on private land outside Greater London, the local authority may impose terms, conditions and restrictions on any licence it issues **only** for certain particular purposes which are specified in paragraph 4(4) of Schedule 1 to the Act. These concern:-

- securing the safety of performers and other people present at the entertainment;

- ensuring there is adequate access for emergency vehicles and provision of sanitary appliances; and

- preventing unreasonable noise disturbance to people in the neighbourhood.

It is, however, possible to impose a variety of terms, conditions or restrictions in respect of an event, provided that they all relate in some way to one of the purposes specified in paragraph 4(4).

Scotland

28 A district or islands council may license public entertainments, including pop concerts, which take place in its area under section 41 of the Civic Government (Scotland) Act 1982 where the particular council has passed a resolution to license a particular class or classes of public entertainment. In such cases, the local authority may grant a public entertainment licence for an event where members of the public attending are required to pay for admission. Where no charge is made the events cannot be licensed under the 1982 Act. Under section 7 of the 1982 Act it is an offence to promote such an event without a licence in circumstances where a licence is required. In granting such a licence, the local authority may attach conditions regulating such matters as the start and finish time of the concert or imposing requirements in respect of tickets, crowd capacity, crowd density and environmental noise levels. Such conditions are designed to ensure that there are adequate standards of public safety with respect to the venue, its contents and fire precautions.

29 A pop concert may also take place on premises for which a licensing board has granted an entertainment licence under the Licensing (Scotland) Act 1976. Such a licence may be granted for places of entertainment such as cinemas, theatres, dance halls and proprietary clubs and permits the sale or supply of liquor for consumption on the premises provided that the sale or supply of liquor is ancillary to the entertainment provided. A licensing board may attach conditions to a licence to ensure that the sale or supply of alcohol is indeed ancillary to the entertainment.

Overlapping legislation

30 Sections 3 & 4 of the HSW Act, because of their wide scope, often overlap with other legislation. The Health and Safety Commission's policy is that, wherever possible, duplication of enforcement should be avoided. In many cases, enforcing authorities have reached agreement that the requirements of Sections 3 and 4 should not be enforced if public safety can be adequately guaranteed by the enforcement of other, more specific, legislation.

31 In relation to pop concerts and similar entertainments, licensing legislation will normally provide powers to make specific requirements and should, in these circumstances, be regarded as the more appropriate legislation.

NOTES/AMENDMENTS

ENFORCEMENT OF HEALTH AND SAFETY LEGISLATION

1 Responsibility for enforcing health and safety legislation in Great Britain is shared by HSE and local authorities. The premises where local authorities are responsible are determined by the Health and Safety (Enforcing Authority) Regulations 1989.

Who enforces?

2 Enforcement responsibility for health and safety legislation is determined on the basis of "main activity". The Health and Safety Commission's policy is that wherever possible health and safety legislation should be enforced in particular premises by one enforcing authority and there are powers which provide a simple administrative procedure to allow transfers between enforcing authorities. In practice, this means that the enforcing authority will be either the Health and Safety Executive or the local authority.

3 Where the "main activity" is a leisure activity (which includes pop concerts), it is the responsibility of the local authority to enforce health and safety legislation, except where the local authority is running the event, when it will be for HSE to enforce. Where a pop concert takes place in part of a larger premises and the normal occupier of the premises is also running the concert, enforcement will be allocated to the authority which normally inspects the rest of the premises.

4 The Enforcing Authority Regulations make provision for certain activities to be enforced by HSE. For a concert, these may include aspects of construction work and radio and television broadcasting. If the concert itself is enforced by the local authority, however, arrangments are often made to transfer responsiblitiy for these activities so that the local authority is responsible for the whole event.

Powers of entry and inspection

5 Health and safety inspectors have statutory powers of entry to relevant premises at all reasonable times. Obstructing an inspector, including inspectors exercising their powers of entry, is a criminal offence under the HSW Act.

6 Inspectors also have enforcement powers, including powers to serve improvement notices, (which may require certain steps to be taken to achieve acceptable levels of health and safety), or prohibition notices, (which can stop a work activity where, in the inspector's opinion, there is imminent risk of serious personal injury). Inspectors also have other statutory powers, including powers to take samples, photographs etc.

7 Failure to comply with an improvement or prohibition notice, or breach of the health and safety legislation, may lead to a criminal prosecution.

NOTES/AMENDMENTS

ACOUSTICAL UNITS AND TERMINOLOGY

1 This appendix describes the main acoustical units used. It is not intended to provide formal definitions, which can be found in the relevant legislation and codes.

Sound waves

2 Airborne sound is transmitted by small pressure fluctuations above and below the normal atmospheric pressure, which radiate away from a source such as a loudspeaker.

Frequency in hertz (Hz)

3 The number of complete pressure fluctuations per second is called the frequency of the sound. The units are cycles per second, or hertz. Most sounds consist of a mixture of frequencies across a broad band.

4 The human ear is most sensitive in the frequency range from about 500 to 5,000 Hz, and progressively less sensitive at higher and lower frequencies. There are considerable individual differences in the frequency limits that people can hear. Young people can hear sound with frequencies ranging from very approximately 25 Hz to 20,000 Hz. With age the ability to hear the higher frequencies falls off.

Sound pressure in pascals (Pa)

5 For most purposes the "root-mean-square" (rms) average magnitude of the pressure fluctuations is measured. Most sound level meters can be set to an "F" (fast) response which averages the pressure over 125 milliseconds, and an "S" (slow) response which averages over about 1 second. For assessing the hazard to hearing, the average over a longer period is also measured, and this is called "equivalent continuous sound level" (see paragraph 11).

6 In the frequency range where the ear is most sensitive, the faintest audible sounds have an rms pressure of about 2×10^{-5} pascals (about 0.00000003 lbs/in^2) and the loudest sounds people can tolerate have an rms pressure of around 10 pascals.

7 Sometimes the peak pressure reached by the sound waves is also needed, usually when assessing the hazard created by a loud sound impulse. Special equipment is needed to measure this.

Sound pressure level (dB)

8 It is usually more convenient to express the large range of sound pressures which can be heard by humans on a logarithmic decibel scale, which compresses the scale to more managable numbers. On this scale the faintest audible sounds have a sound pressure level of about 0 dB, and the loudest tolerable sounds have a sound pressure level of about 120 dB. The logarithmic scale also corresponds approximately with the way the ear responds to the apparent loudness of sounds. On this scale:-

- each 3 dB increase in sound pressure level represents a doubling of the sound energy being transmitted by the sound waves. A listener would, however, notice only a small change in loudness; and

- each 10 dB increase in pressure level represents a tenfold increase in the sound energy being transmitted. Most listeners would judge the loudness to be about doubled.

A-weighted sound pressure level (dB(A))

9 Because the ear is not equally sensitive to all frequencies it is convenient to measure noise using an instrument which responds to the whole of the audible frequency range, but which contains a filter or "A-weighting network" which reduces the meter's response to low and very high frequency sound where the ear is less sensitive. This system is used for assessing both the loudness of sound and its potential for causing hearing damage. Measurements made using this filter are given as "dB(A)".

10 Many sound level meters also have other weighting networks ("B", "C", and "D") but they have a limited use for assessing the hazard to hearing. The "C" network is sometimes used for measuring the peak sound pressure of noise impulses.

Equivalent continuous sound level (L$_{Aeq}$)

11 This is the rms average of the A-weighted sound pressure level over a relatively long period (usually several hours). It is expressed as a decibel value. Instruments for measuring the L$_{Aeq}$ are usually designed so that the operator can decide when to start and stop the averaging process.

Event equivalent continuous sound level (Event L$_{Aeq}$)

12 The value of the L$_{Aeq}$ is determined by measuring from the start of the first act to the end of the last act.

Daily personal exposure to noise (L$_{EP,d}$)

13 This is used in the Noise at Work Regulations as a measure of the total sound exposure a person receives during the day. It is formally defined in the Schedule to the Regulations.

14 L$_{EP,d}$ is determined taking into account the various A-weighted sound levels (dB(A)) a person is exposed to and how long he or she is exposed to them, but taking no account of any ear protection worn. Its value will depend on the L$_{Aeq}$ over the exposure period and the length of the exposure period. For example, Table 3 shows how long people could be exposed at various levels before they reach an $L_{EP,d}$ of 9o dB(A).

Table 3   Noise exposure time

L_{Aeq} over exposure period	Exposure time to reach an $L_{EP,d}$ of 90 dB(A)
87 dB(A)	16 hours
90 dB(A)	8 hours
93 dB(A)	4 hours
96 dB(A)	2 hours
108 dB(A)	7½ minutes

Ear protectors

15   Ear muffs or ear plugs are used to protect the ears against high sound levels. The amount by which ear protectors reduce the sound reaching the ear (the attenuation) will depend on the design of the protector and the frequency of the sound. When selecting protectors, the aim is to match the amount of attenuation to the loudness of the sound.

16   Protectors are usually most effective at high frequencies. The supplier can normally provide tables of attenuation at different frequencies determined from the standard test procedure set out in Britain Standard 5108 and International Standard (ISO) 4869.

17   HSE's guidance (Noise Guide No 5) describes how a value of "assumed protection" at each test frequency can be calculated from the test data. This is the amount of protection most people should receive if the protectors are properly fitted and in good condition. Most suppliers can also supply this information about their products. The assumed protection can be used to calculate whether the ear muffs or plugs will give adequate protection against the sound exposure.

18   Ear protectors with the assumed protection figures below will provide adequate protection for most areas at pop concerts.

Table 4   Assumed protection figures

Frequency – Hz	63	125	250	500	1,000 (1k)	2,000 (2k)
Assumed protection – dB	14	17	17	17	18	>25

NOTES/AMENDMENTS

142

CHECK LIST OF ITEMS FOR POP CONCERTS

Venue ....Date ....

Address ....

....

Telephone No .... Telex No .... Fax No ....

Contact points

Names/Addresses	Tel/Fax No

1   Venue owner.

2   Event organiser/promoter.

3   Licensing authority or officer.

4   Health and safety enforcement officer.

5   Police.

6   Fire authority.

7   NHS ambulance

8   First aid organisation.

9   Public transport organisation.

10   Site personnel.

     ....

     ....

     (a)   Manager.

     (b)   Chief steward.

     (c)   Scaffolding company.

     (d)   Sound engineer.

     (e)   Lighting rig.

     (f)   Electrical services.

     (g)   Sanitary facilities/washing facilities.

     (h)   Merchandising.

     (i)   Crew catering.

     (j)   Food and drink concessionaires.

     (k)   Car/coach parking.

     (l)   Refuse. Skip, contractor/site cleaning.

     (m)   Video screen operator.

(n) Pyrotechnician.

(o) Laser operator.

Action list: suggested items for inclusion

1   Site drawings, including parking arrangements.

2   Stage drawings. { } Test figures: loadings & wind tests

Mixer - tower. { } Test figures: loadings & wind tests

Delay - tower { } Test figures: loadings & wind tests

Platforms for people wtih disabilities. { } Test figures: loadings & wind tests

Videoscreen and platform { } Test figures: loadings & wind tests

3   Structural engineer – Documents sent .... Date ....

Observations received .... Date ....

4   Machinery test certificates.

5   Generators – Certificate No – 3 Phase /RCD/Earth spike/Earth loop monitor/ Cable routes – Ducts /Covers/Buried.

6   Fire retardancy test certificates.

7   Smoke machines – Certificates.

8   Pyrotechnics – Approval by licensing authority.

9   Lasers. Certificate No .... PM.19.

Other checks:

10   Water supply to pit area – taps/cups.

11   Front of stage barrier – design/loadings.

12   Number of stewards, including register report time, briefing and high visibility clothing.

13   Fire points including stage and backstage area.

14   (a) Pressurised gas containers, including the siting of apparatus.

(b) LPG storage – siting of compound and location of vendors.

15   Incident control centre.

16   Communications/PA/loud hailers.

17   Signage – public highway
               – venue

18   Public transport – signage/pedestrian access/public boarding points.

19   Entrances – turnstiles/counters/barriers/opening time.

20   First aid locations/medical centre/telephones/drinking water/toilets/power/ lighting/doctors/ambulances/hospital.

21   Sanitary accommodation and washing facilities.

WCs/urinals/wash-hand basins
disabled facilities/crew
construction and maintenance.

23   Noise control.

Monitoring points/power supply, equipment/staff/limit

24   Security fences – perimeter/backstage area/type/lifting equipment on site

NOTES/AMENDMENTS

Printed in the United Kingdom for The Stationery Office
J59846 C10 9/98